I0419200

Copyright 2019 by Artvoices Art Books

All rights reserved; no portion of this work may be reproduced
without the permission of the publisher and or artist.

LCCN: 2019952489

ISBN: 978-1-7320048-0-1

Printed in China

Designed by Jen Zhao

First Artvoices Art Books Publishing edition 2019

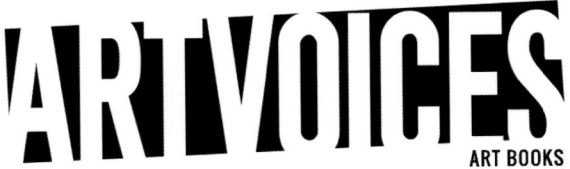

Artvoices Art Books Publishing
www.artvoicesartbooks.com

Home. In my heart, beating far away.

LALI KHALID

Essays by Professor Allen Frame and Professor Jaspal Kaur Singh

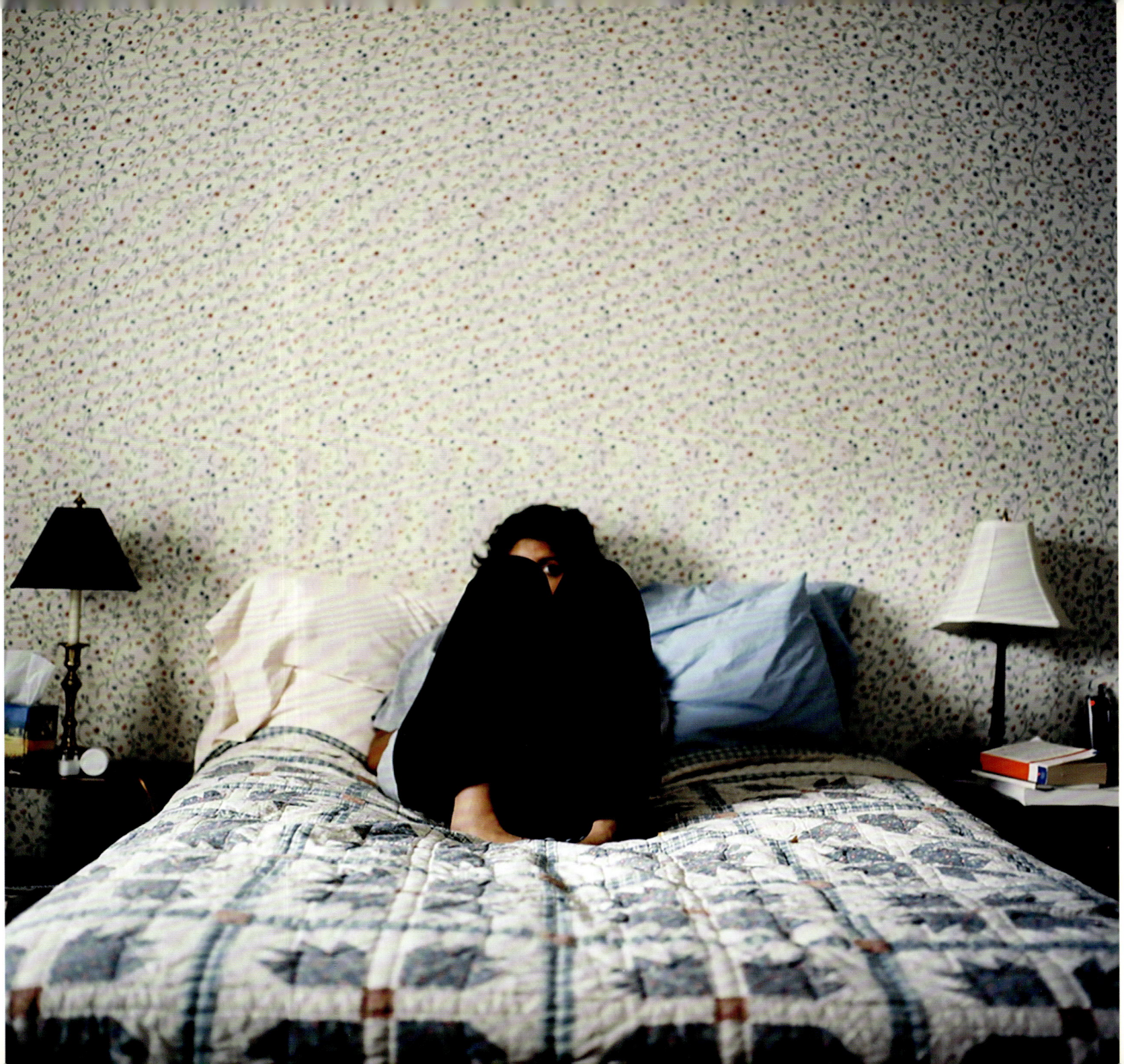

For my son Azan, who gives me strength every day, and without whom this book would not be possible.

Thank you, Amma & Baba, for your unfaltering support.

INTRODUCTION

Set Free

by Professor Allen Frame

Lali Khalid's photographs of herself, her son, and close family members, evoke the uncertain and alienating experience of being an immigrant, away from family and culture, a situation in her case that is mitigated by the pleasure and rewards of independence and motherhood. The veil, or mask, is the unifying element in the series; it references, of course, her Muslim upbringing in Pakistan, and the tension between that tradition and the contemporary world, whether in Pakistan or the U.S. where she now lives, makes art, teaches, and rears a child. The photographs, made over ten years, trace the changing sense of vitality and freedom in her life; light and shadow mediate these shifts. That her face is hidden in shadow is a metaphor for its being veiled, of not being fully realized or independent, whether covered by cloth or psychologically constrained. Many of the pictures are situated in domestic space and feel highly personal, but others are in public space and reflect a broader context.

The book opens with a brooding sequence of photographs in which the artist is seen half in shadow. A certain moody light is itself the subject of one image in which she is absent, but most of the images are self-portraits, a genre in photography that has been particularly accommodating to women, from the early 20th century photographs by Claude Cahun to the much later photos by Cindy Sherman. Mostly when we encounter artists' self-portraits, they are performative, often involving fantasies and masquerades. Using the self as model, artists have commented on the role of women in society, whether with the gender fluidity of Cahun or the chameleon bravura of Sherman's film stills. In Khalid's work, however, the content is closer to home, about self, imparted with a kind of psychological realism. The images are barometers of mood and feeling in particular moments as a register of how it is for the artist to negotiate her life in both the domestic and public spheres.

Light can be concealing but soft and lyrical, as when it falls upon the empty wall of a room. The darkness masking the figure in any number of frames does not have to be read as disturbing, but it does create a dramatic mood and implies, since the context is autobiographical, some particular anxiety in the artist's life. These dark pictures lead into ones in the clear bright light of the outdoors, where we find her in two images that anticipate her pregnancy: one in which her hand rests on her slightly protruding stomach as she lies on a playground sliding board, then one with a fuller stomach standing in the waves on a beach. When

her child appears, he is just partially seen, his head sticking out from behind a large scarf, the "veiling" of the mother imbued on the son, followed by a series of pictures of him that follow his progression into childhood.

A posed family portrait with mother and sister creates a sense of both solidarity and tradition.

Then a magical series begins in which the idea of the veil is made literal and set free, with various pieces of fabric, or dopattas, tossed in the air in a range of situations. Like the film narrative of the "red balloon," whose roaming creates a narrative, the suspension of different pieces of cloth in the air suggests changing conditions and states of mind, from the whimsical, playful, and absurd, to the menacing (above a caution sign), a dark shape that looks like a bird of prey, and to the banal. Changing the

photo language from the psychological to the conceptual, these images depict a procession of mood shifts denoting the vagaries of her existence. There is a sense of optimism, as if a desired change would follow upon a new set of circumstances, but instead, the pieces of cloth, like clouds or shadows or thought balloons, end, and we are back in the anxiety of coping, with signs of worry and confrontation— through court proceedings and darker moods which extend to the images of the child, who is now more often seen in the same dramatic, concealing light with which we were introduced to his mother. In one of the last ones, he has caught his head in her black t-shirt that covers the whole contours of his face. He has become an extension of her; metaphorically, her constraints are now his.

FOREWORD

Never Too Far From Her Watchful Gaze

by Professor Jaspal Kaur Singh

Lali Khalid, a diasporic Punjabi Muslim, a daughter, a mother, an artist, reflects her migrations, fragmentation, alienation, and belonging through solitary or familial images with the overarching theme of the presence and absence of the dupatta, the chunni, or the odhni, a covering, a veil, a protection, sometimes touching her shadowed body, sometimes hovering in the background and sometimes covering her head or partially obscuring her face, and sometimes, absent, lost, or willfully discarded. Symbolizing the theme of journeys and movements, of loss of identity and the recreation of new ones, Khalid integrates plentitude in the image of her small son who, in the initial shots, is her mirror image and close to her body, but through time and space, stands in isolation, beseeching her simultaneously for protection and independence, but he is never too far from her watchful gaze.

The diasporic move from one continent to another, from one cultural space to another, the simultaneous sense of displacement and of belongings are reflected in many of the shots: Khalid, returning the gaze back to the dominant spaces of the US or Pakistan, whether she is in the fields, by the tires, or by the railway tracks. The images are ambiguously placed, as they are simultaneously bright or dark, signifying both expansion and loss—she is self-reflexive as a mother with her small son in the pool, she is sitting isolated and apprehensive in a courthouse, she is prayerful in a green head scarf, she is forever aware of the loss of culture and identity, yet she has

agency for, although she is an immigrant and a Muslim in a post 9/11 world, she reconstructs her identity as empowering through remembrance, in the images of her sister and mother, or through the act of emerging from darkness with a white cotton top, or her son, sitting in the circle of her arms, looking directly at the camera—she is forever rebuilding and recreating her identity as an South Asian American in the private and public spaces of the nation.

Khalid shows her hybrid and fragmented sense of identity, a Pakistani woman in America, an Asian American, a single mother, an artist appearing prayerful in darkness and submission or resistant and revolutionary, an immigrant in the cultural spaces of the nations, Pakistan and the US; yet, even through immigrant loss and wounding, she looks resolutely

and straightforward, intently into the future, subverting stereotypes, charting new horizons and spaces, finding light in the darkest places—her work is illuminating and hopeful—whether her face emerges from the darkness, from behind the fence, or from the shadows and light of the window shades, her eyes are alight and her face shows a strength of purpose and determination. Khalid, a diasporic Pakistani, redefines her gender, cultural and racial identity as an artist, and she is home, wherever she is.

Home. In my heart, beating far away.

LALI KHALID

Essays by Professor Allen Frame and Professor Jaspal Kaur Singh

CHAPTER I

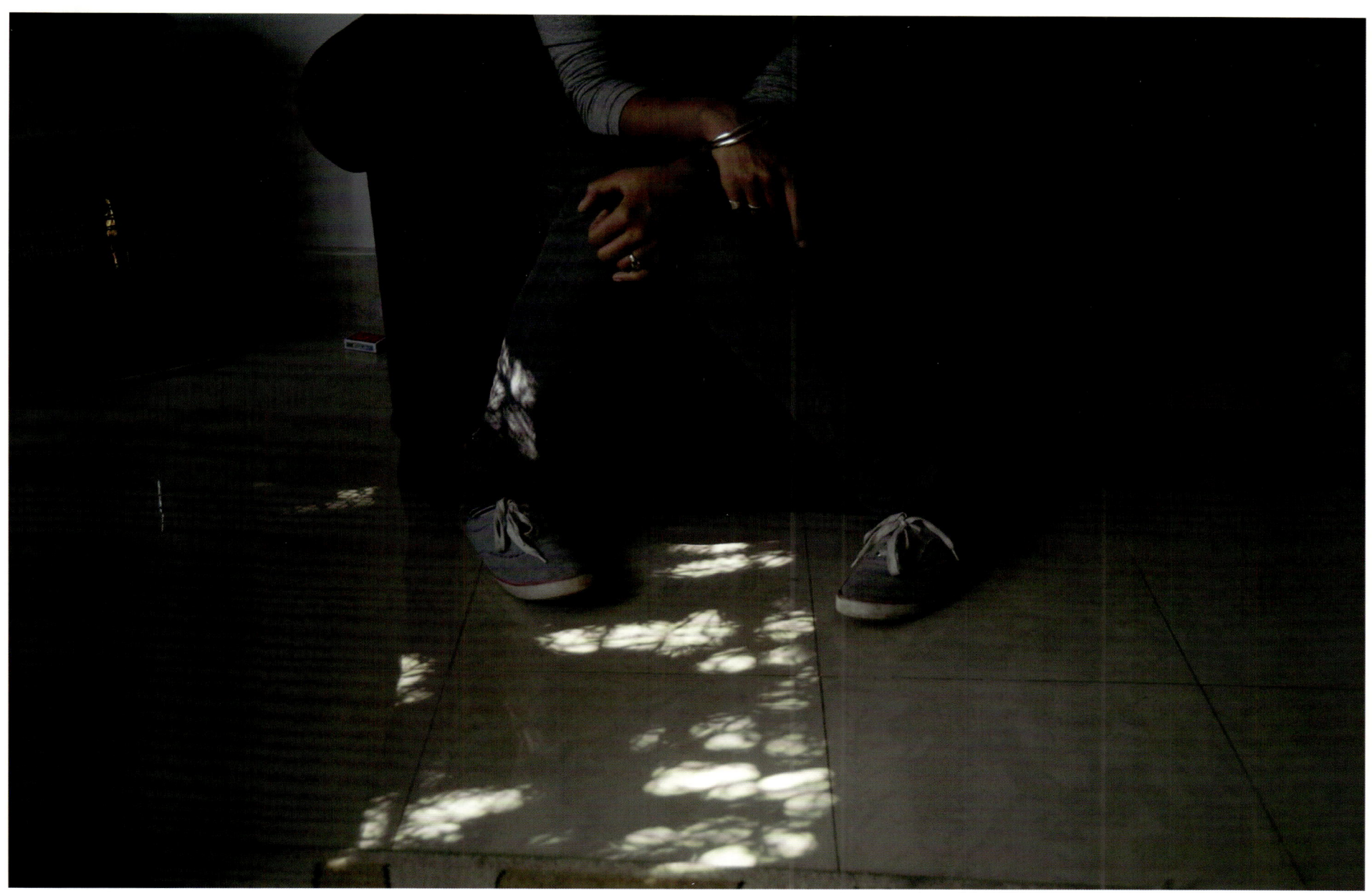

As the shadows get longer

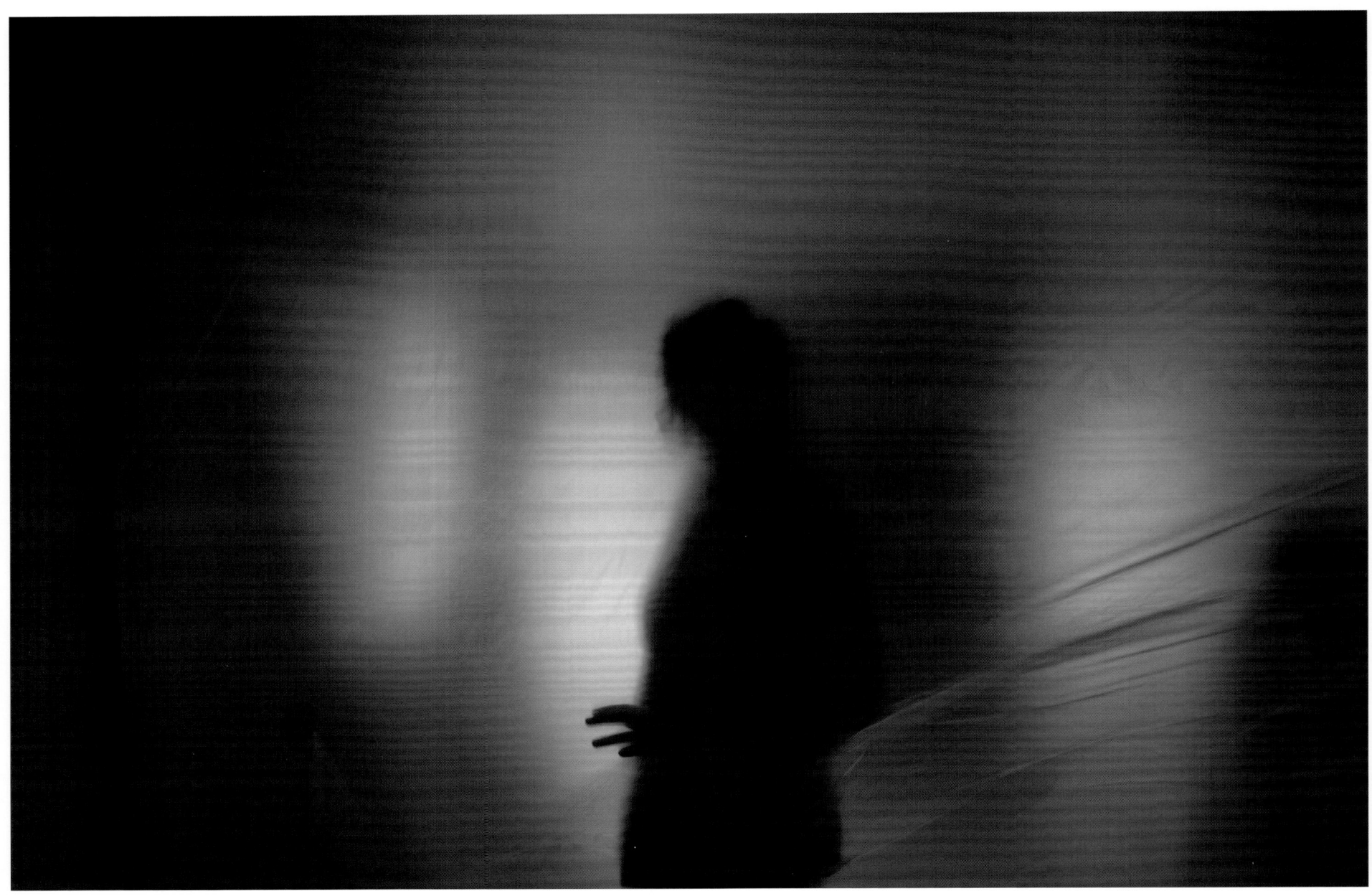

Between you and impossibility

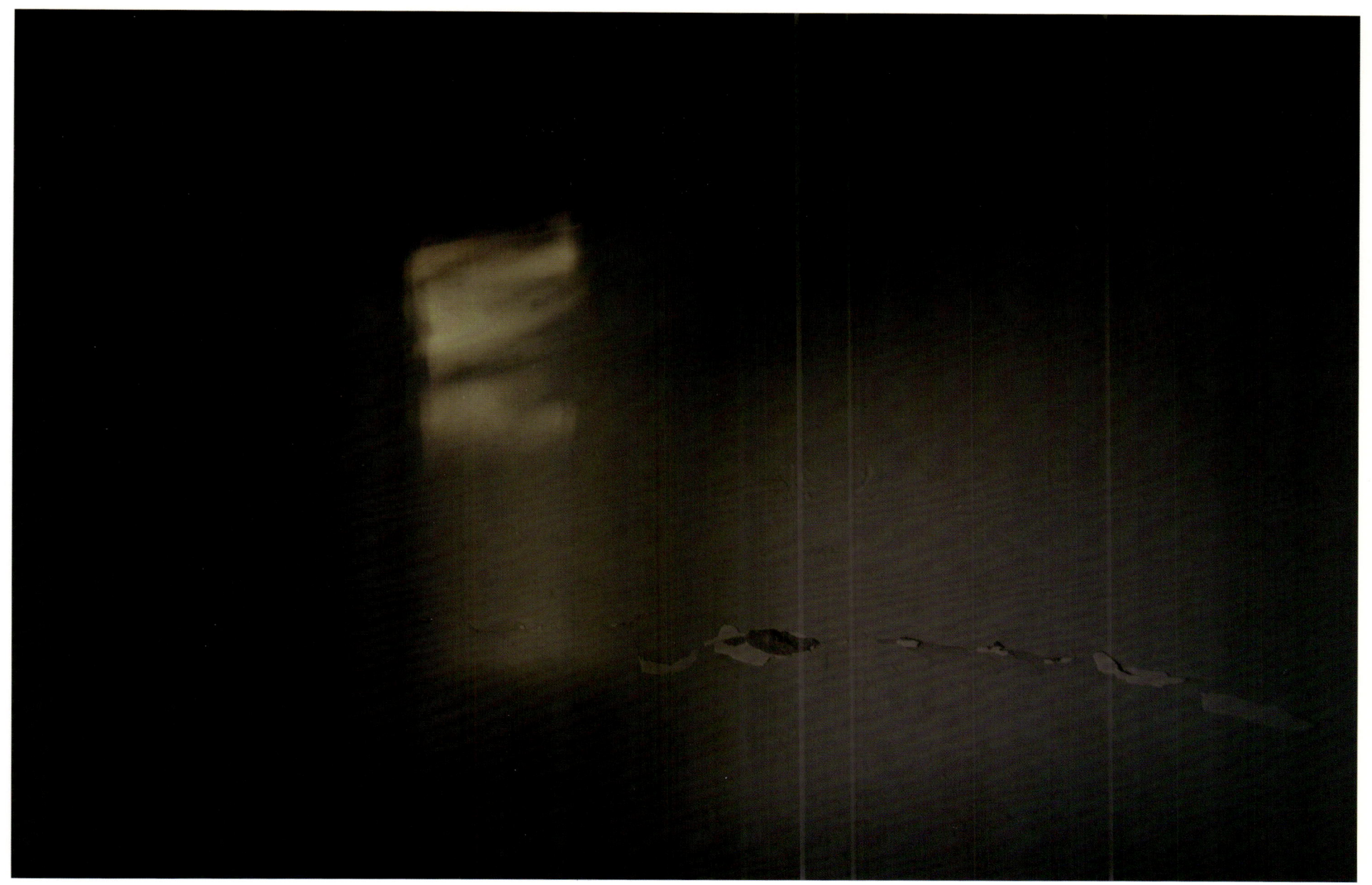

Perhaps the roses really want to grow

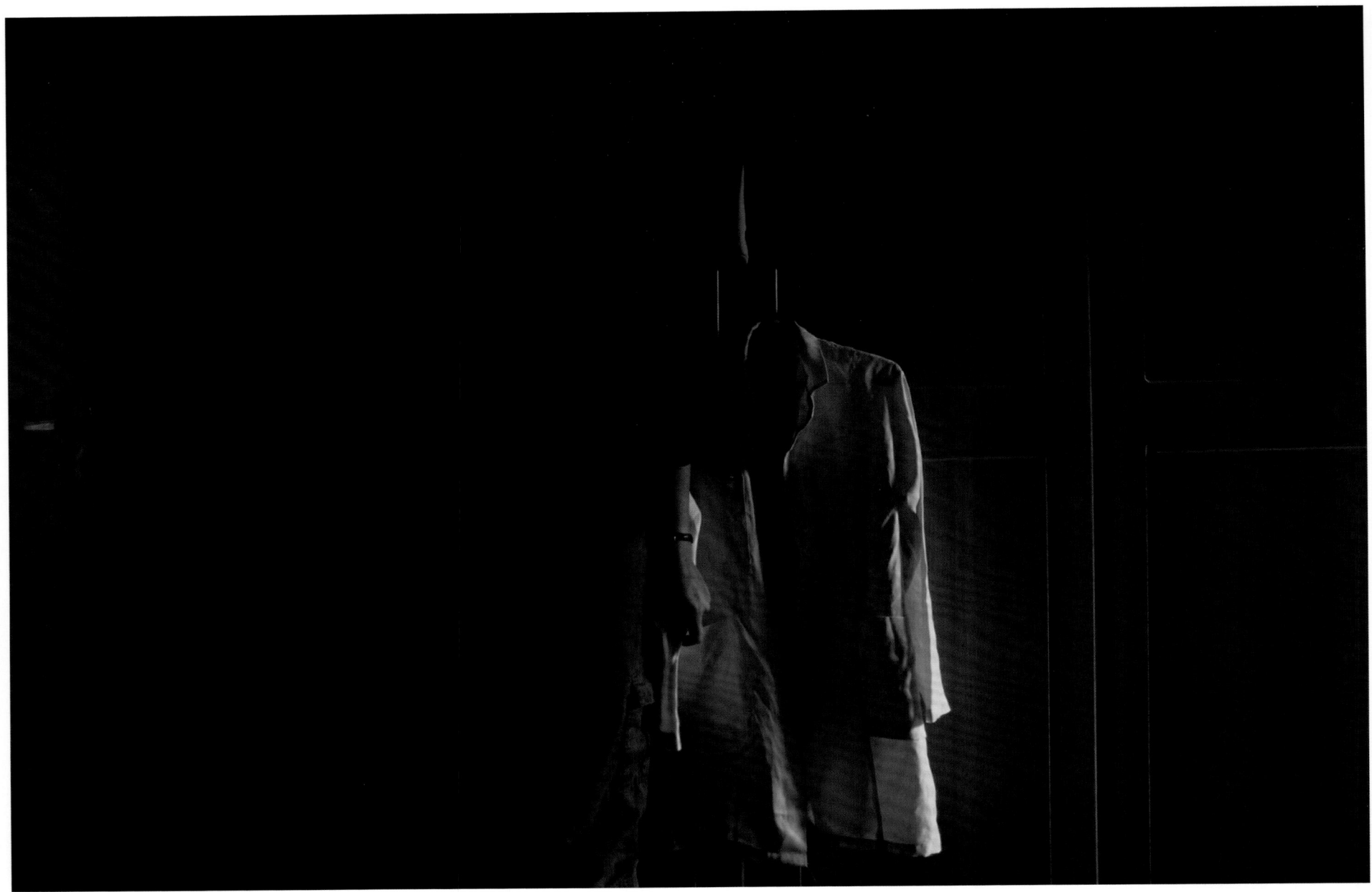

Up in the clouds

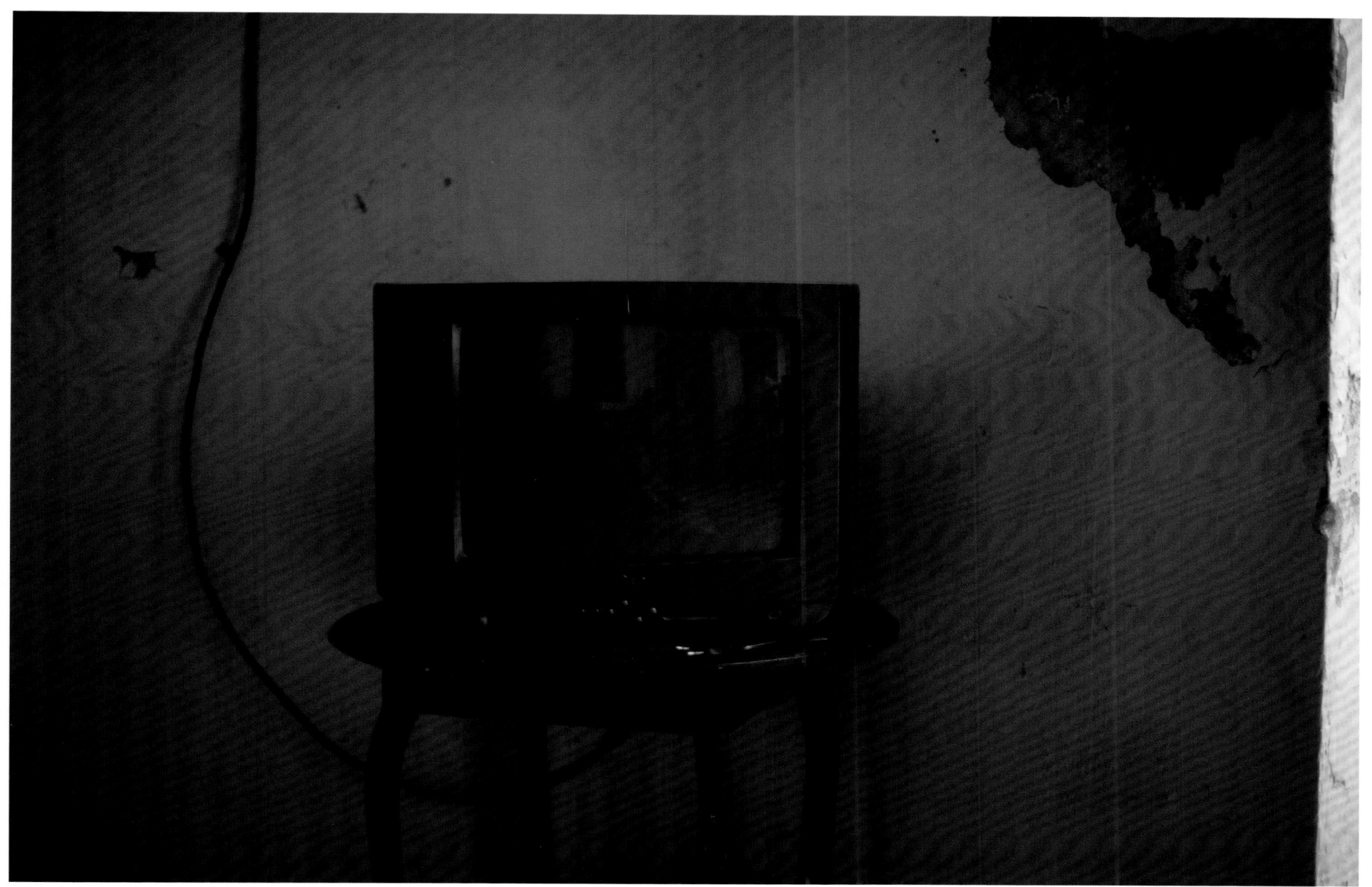

In my medicine cabinet, the winter fly has died of old age

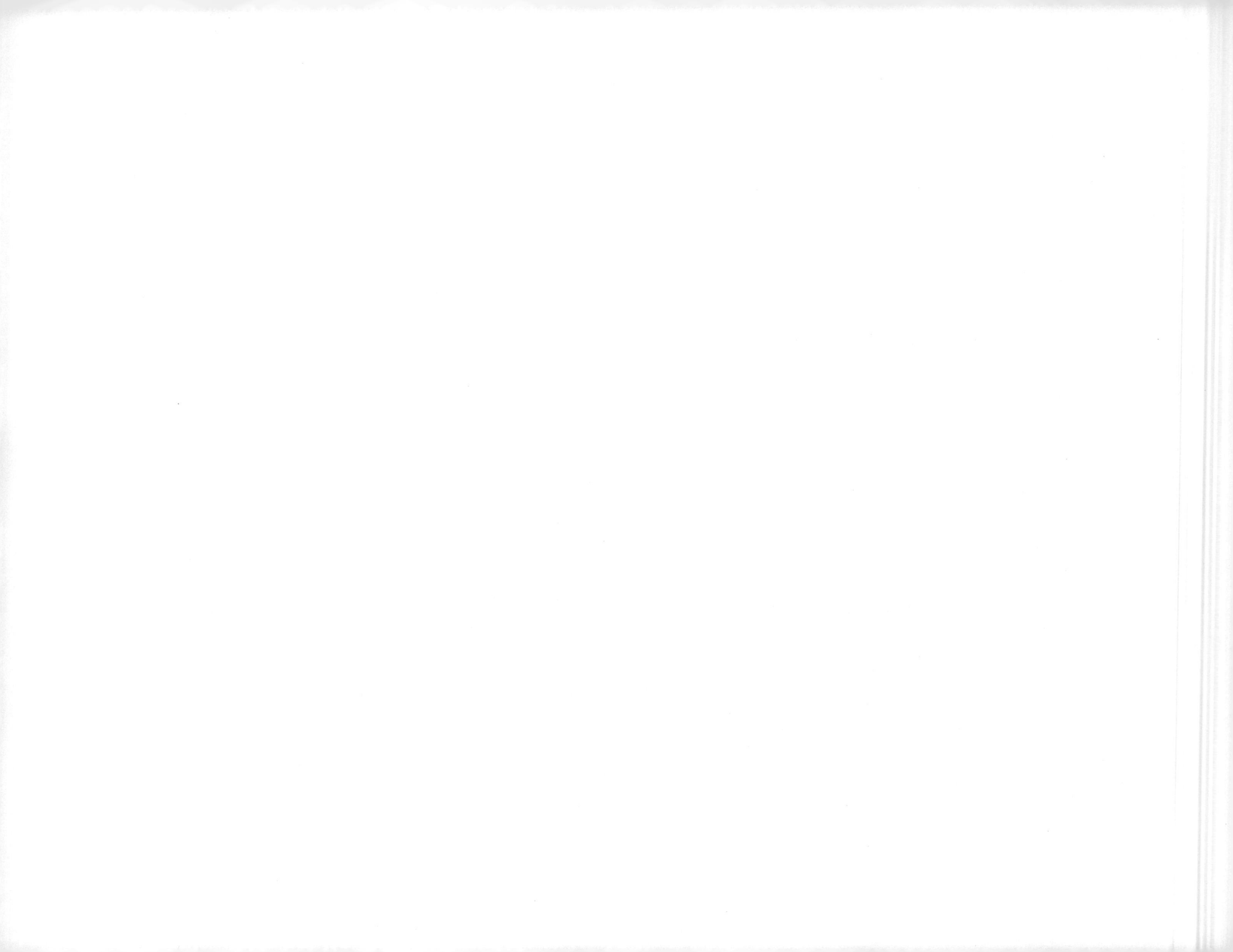

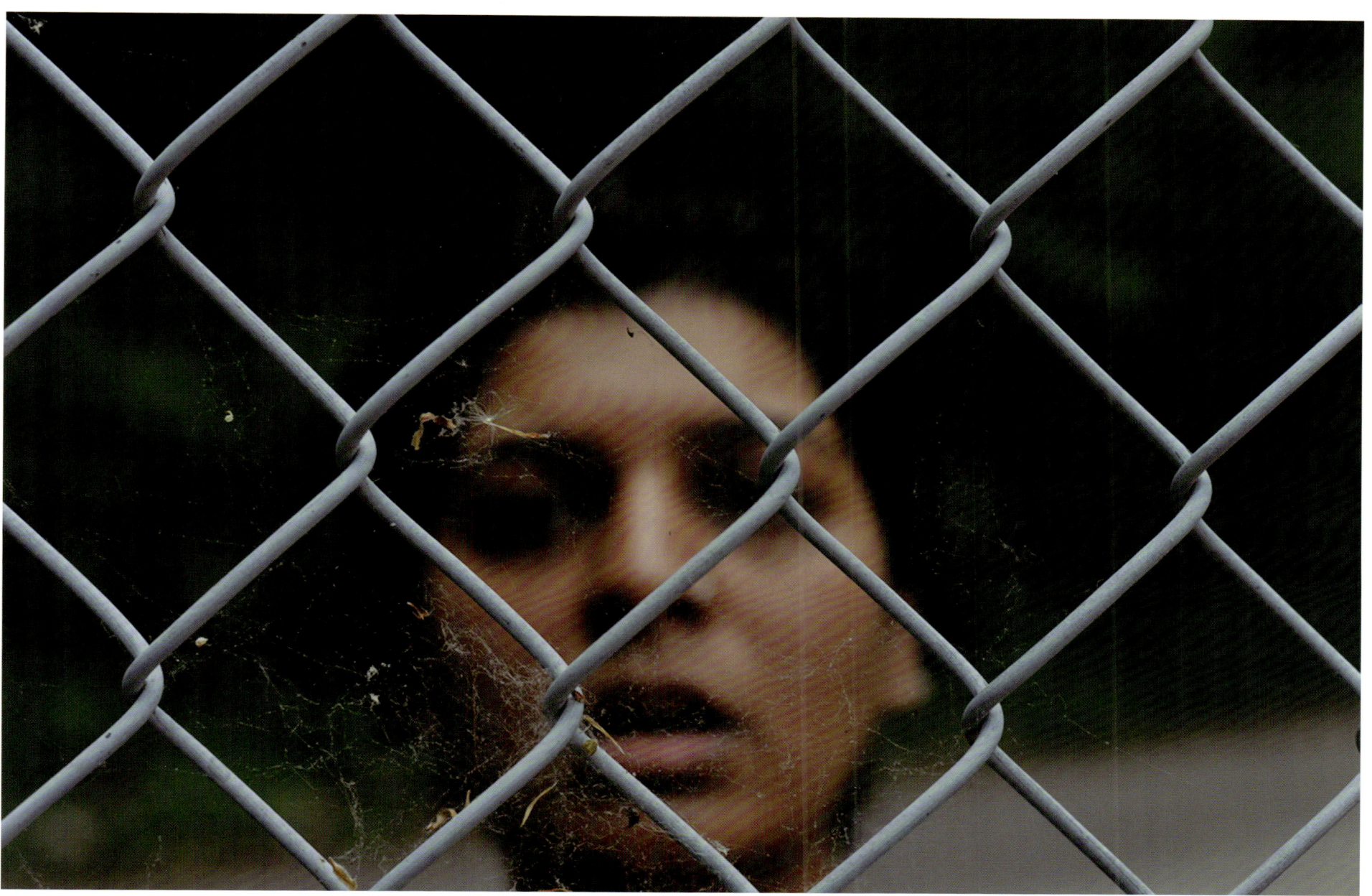

Absurd words

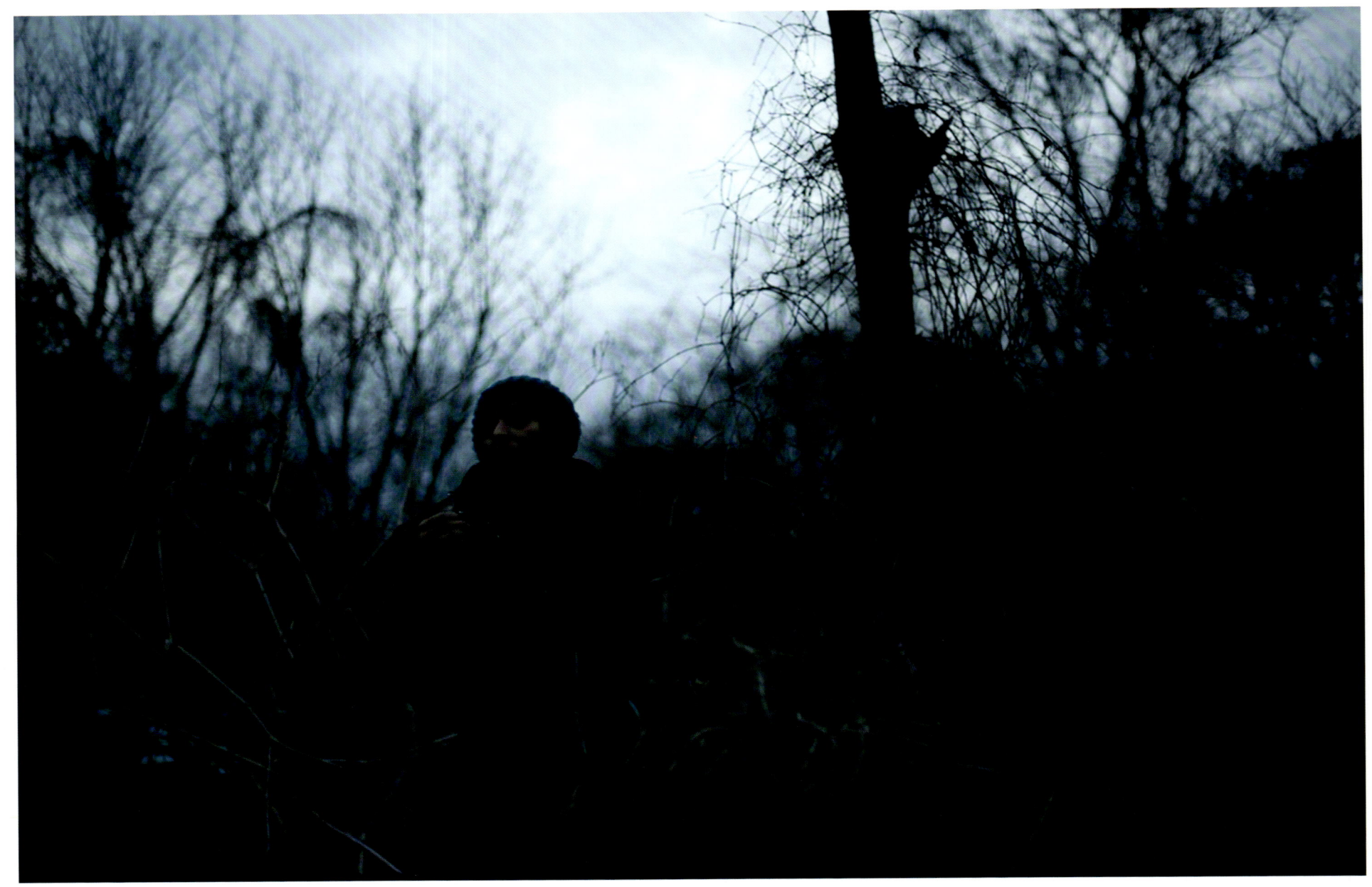

Through wire and fog and dog bark

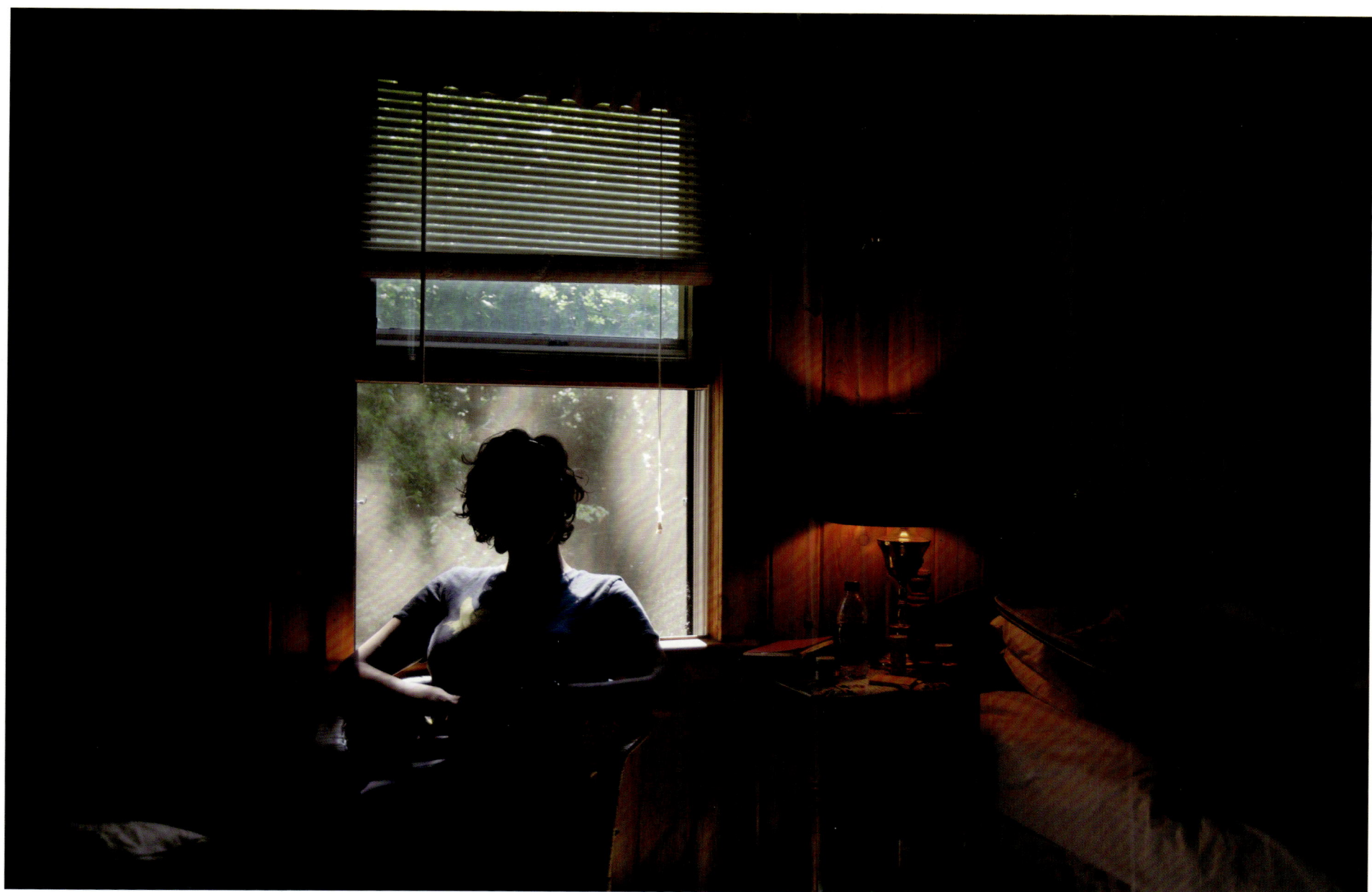

On the last day

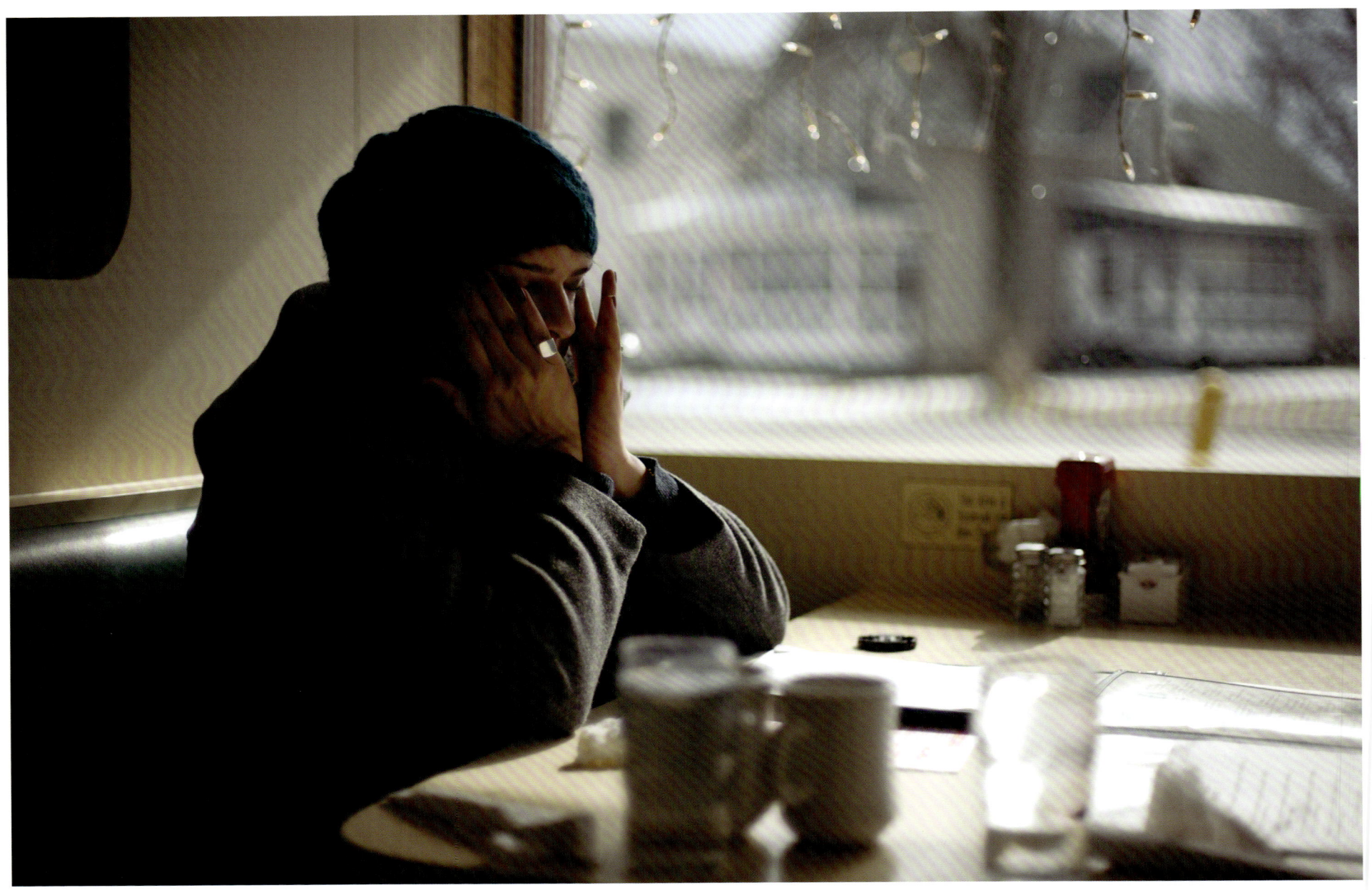

Gathered safely in

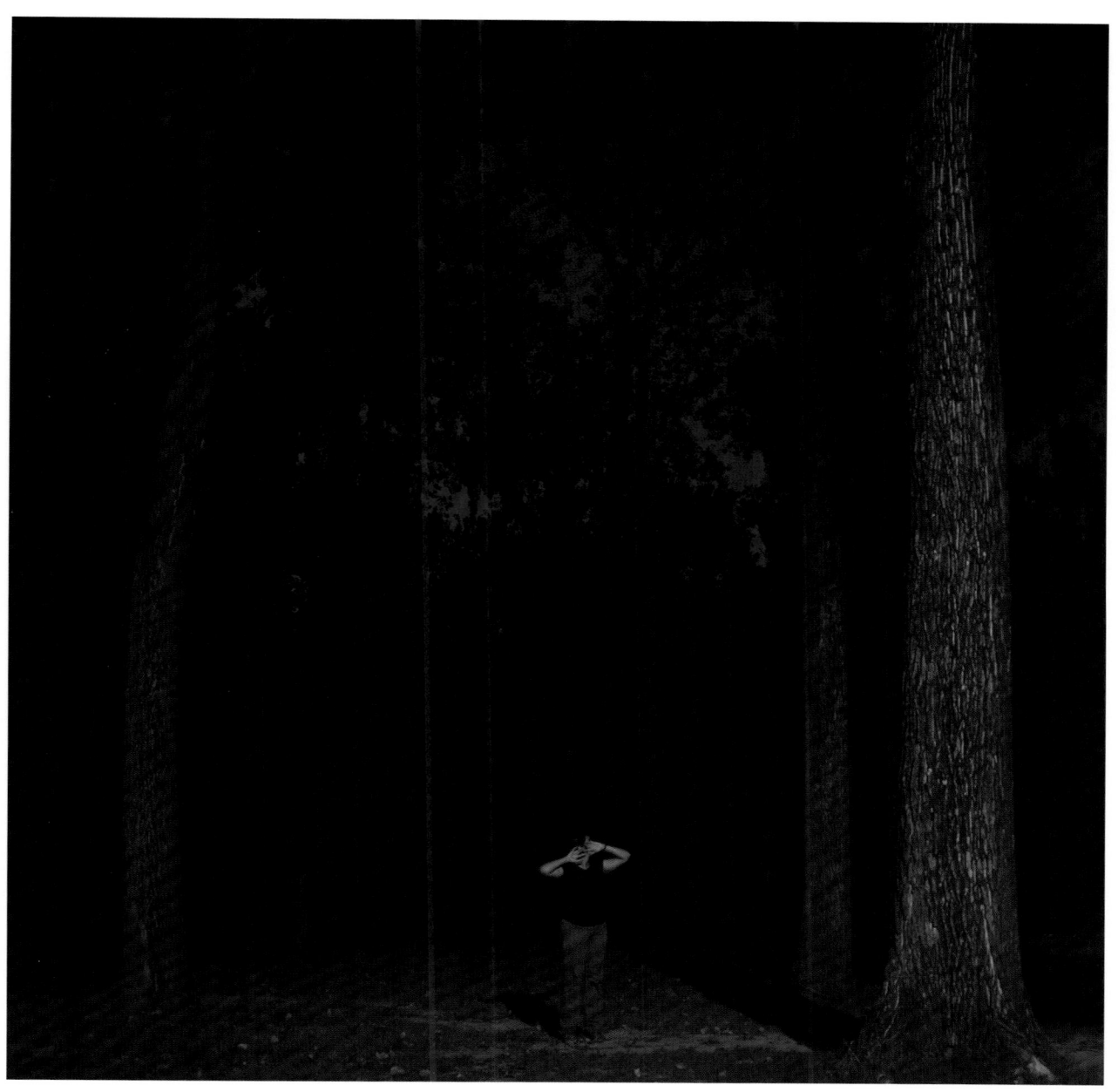

Gulps from the outside in

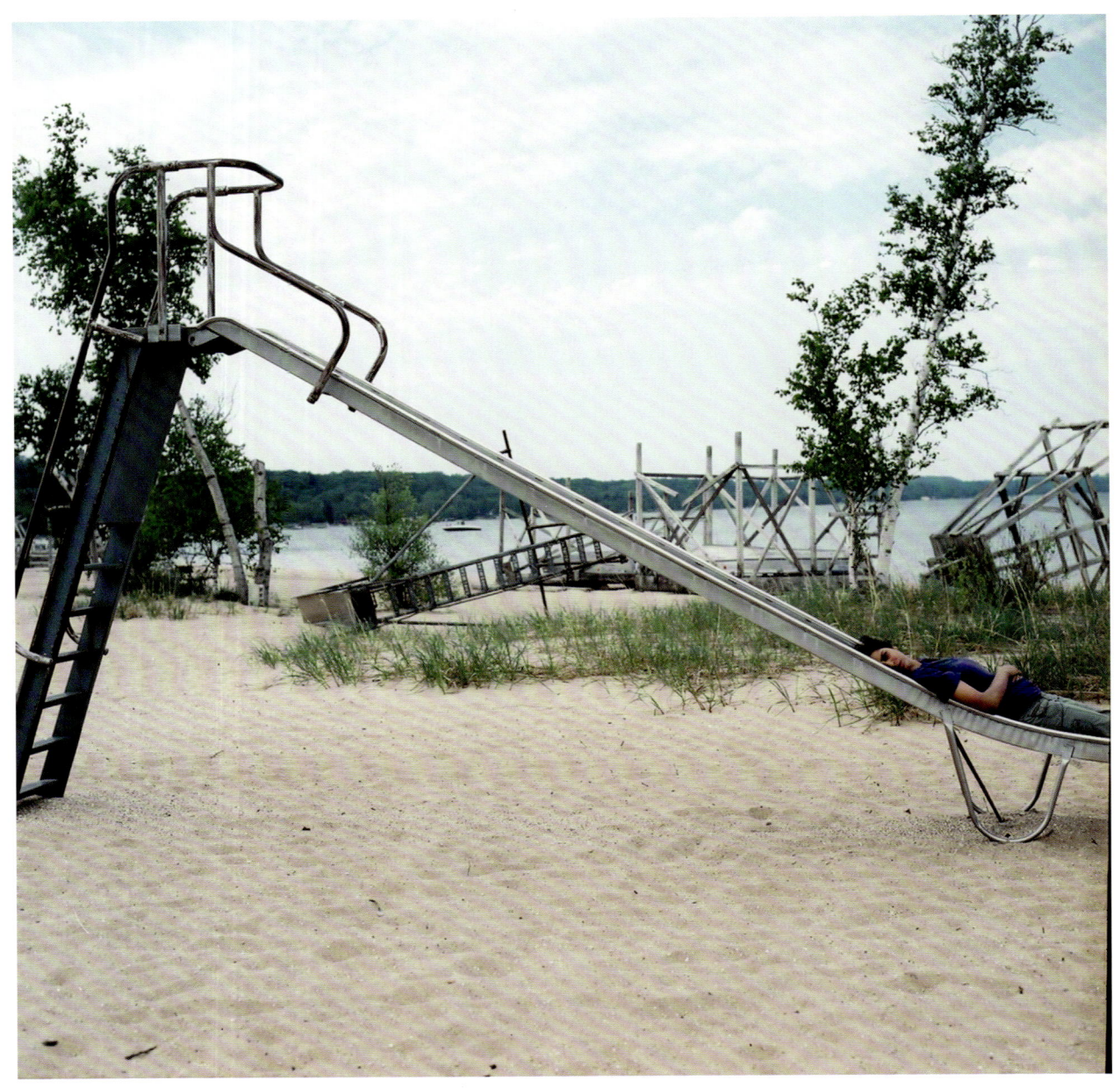

Like the house dropping in the sea

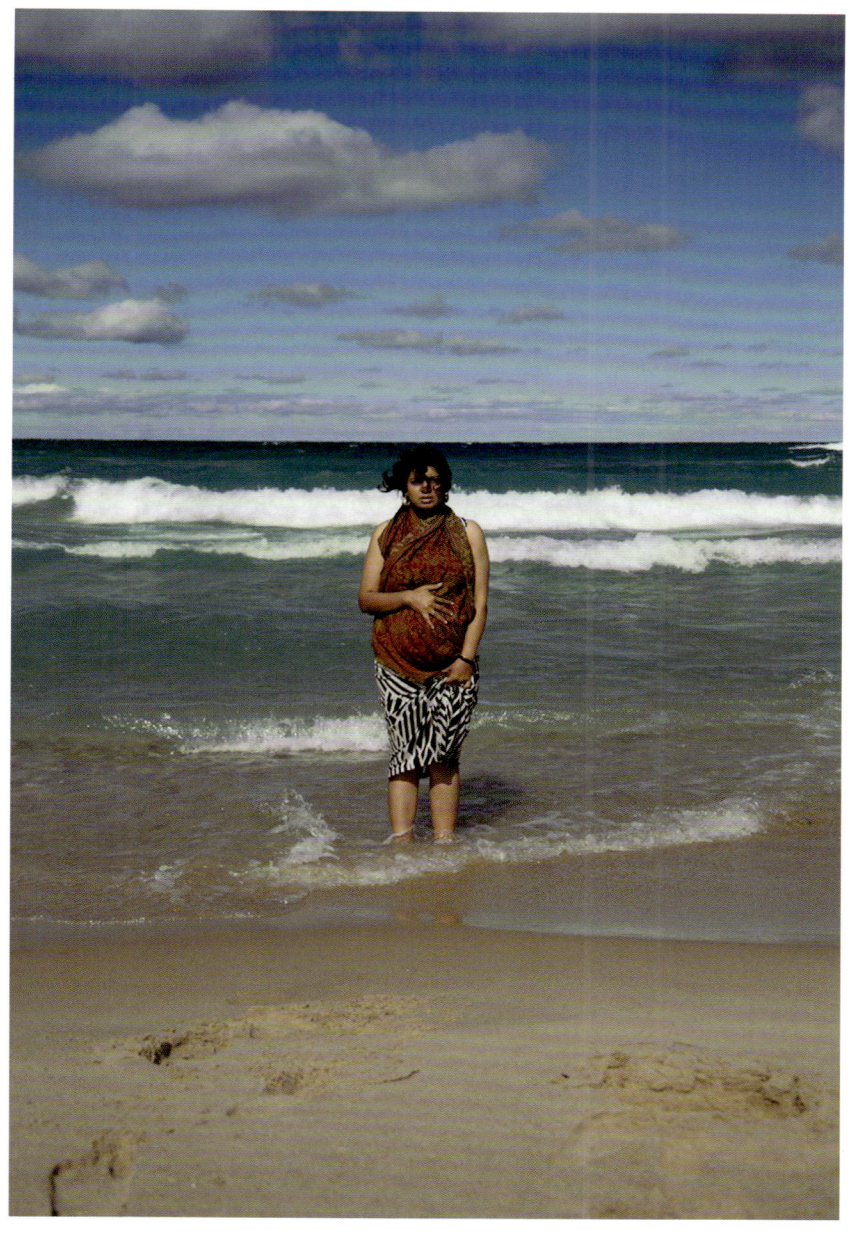

Center within the center

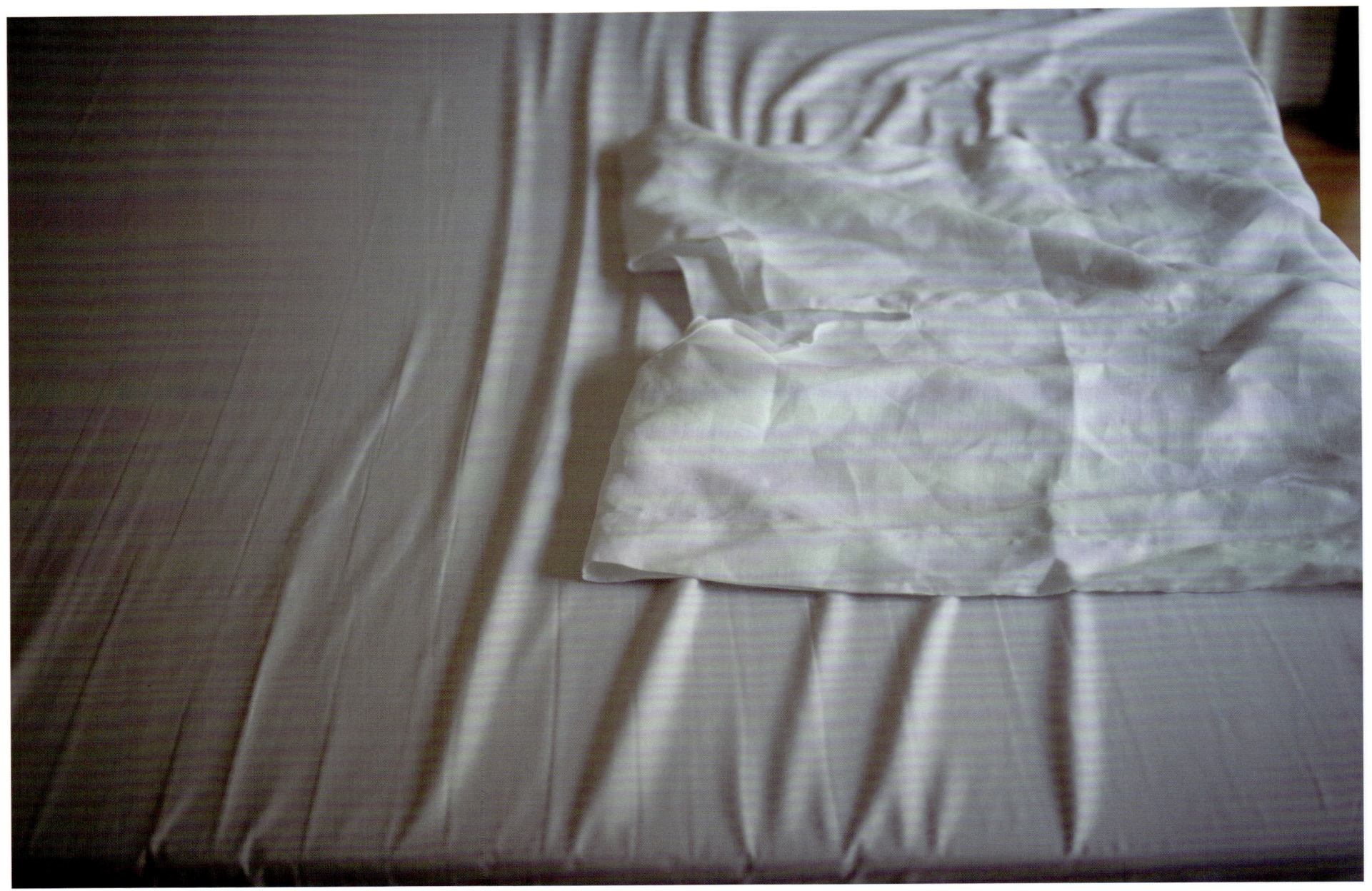

Spiraling down

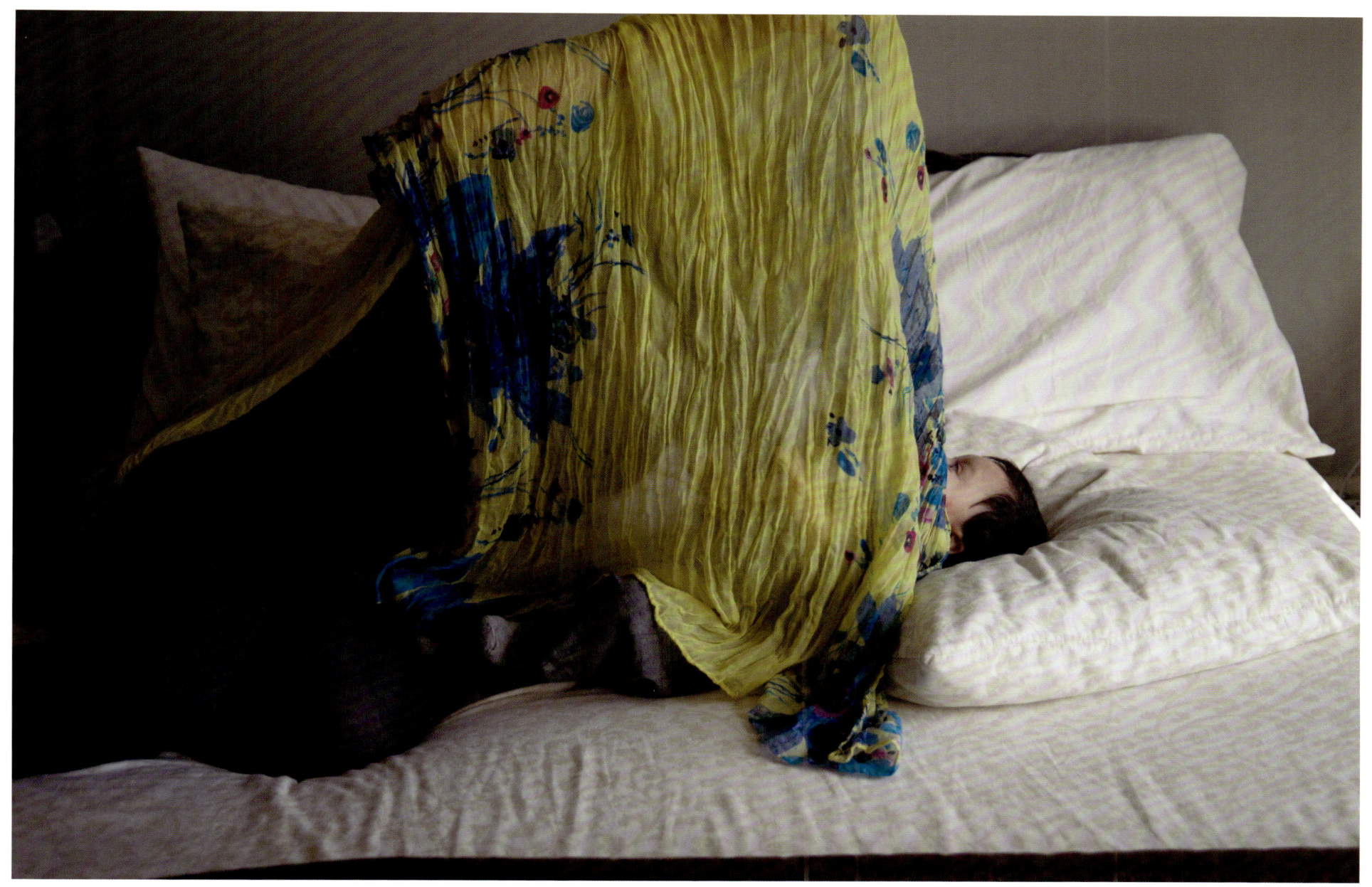

Only seeking

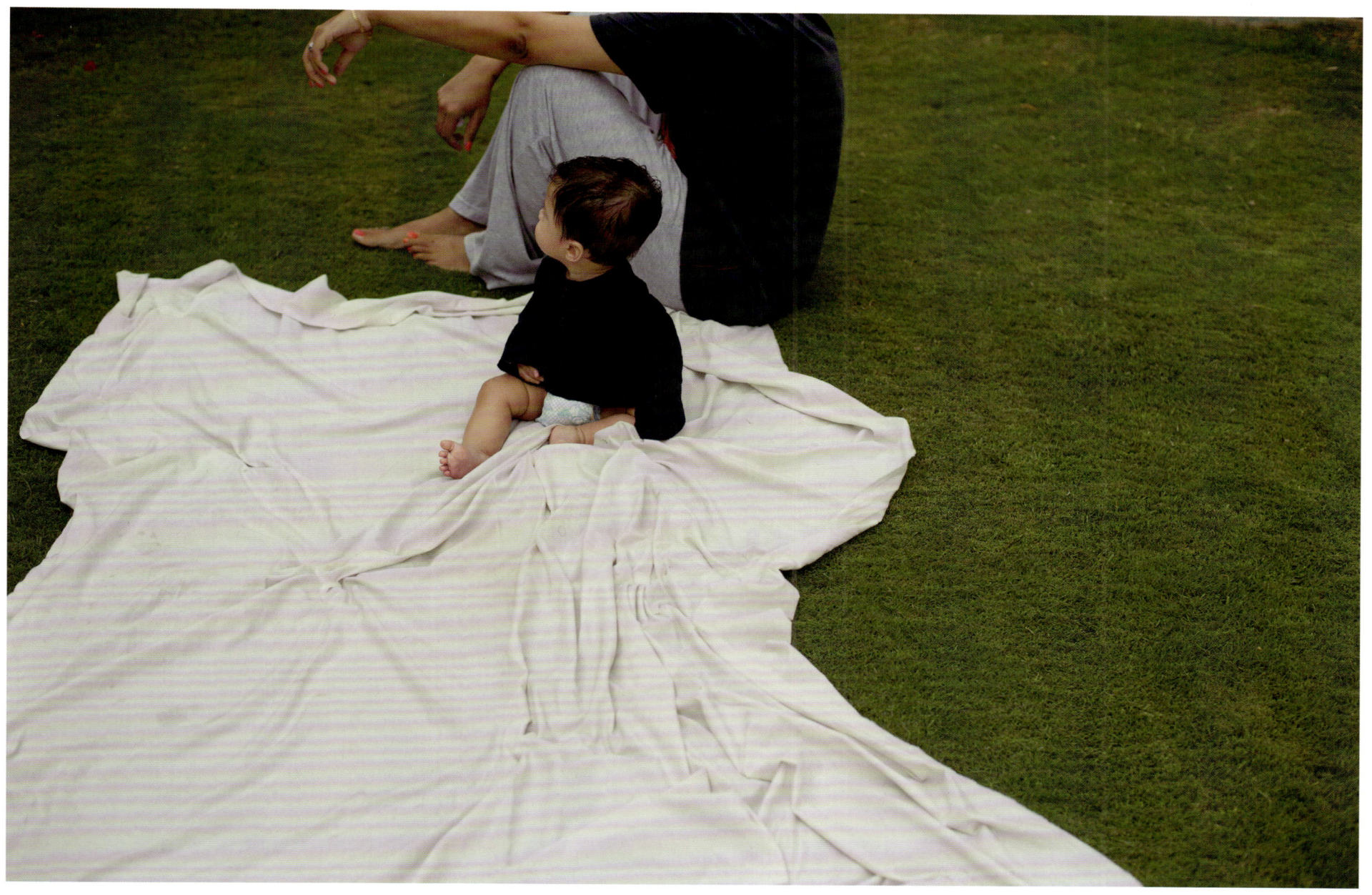

Something to do

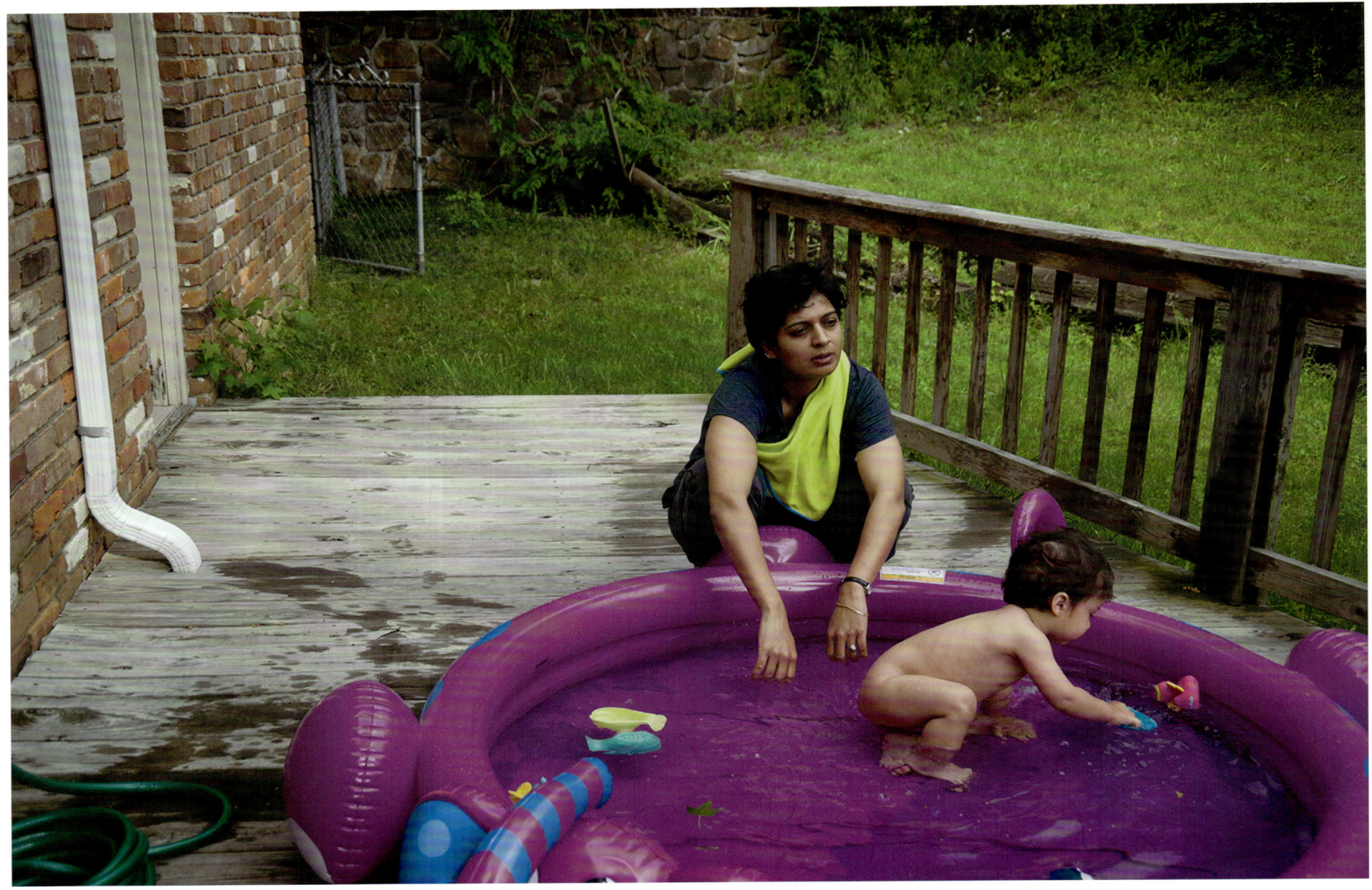

A summer that was

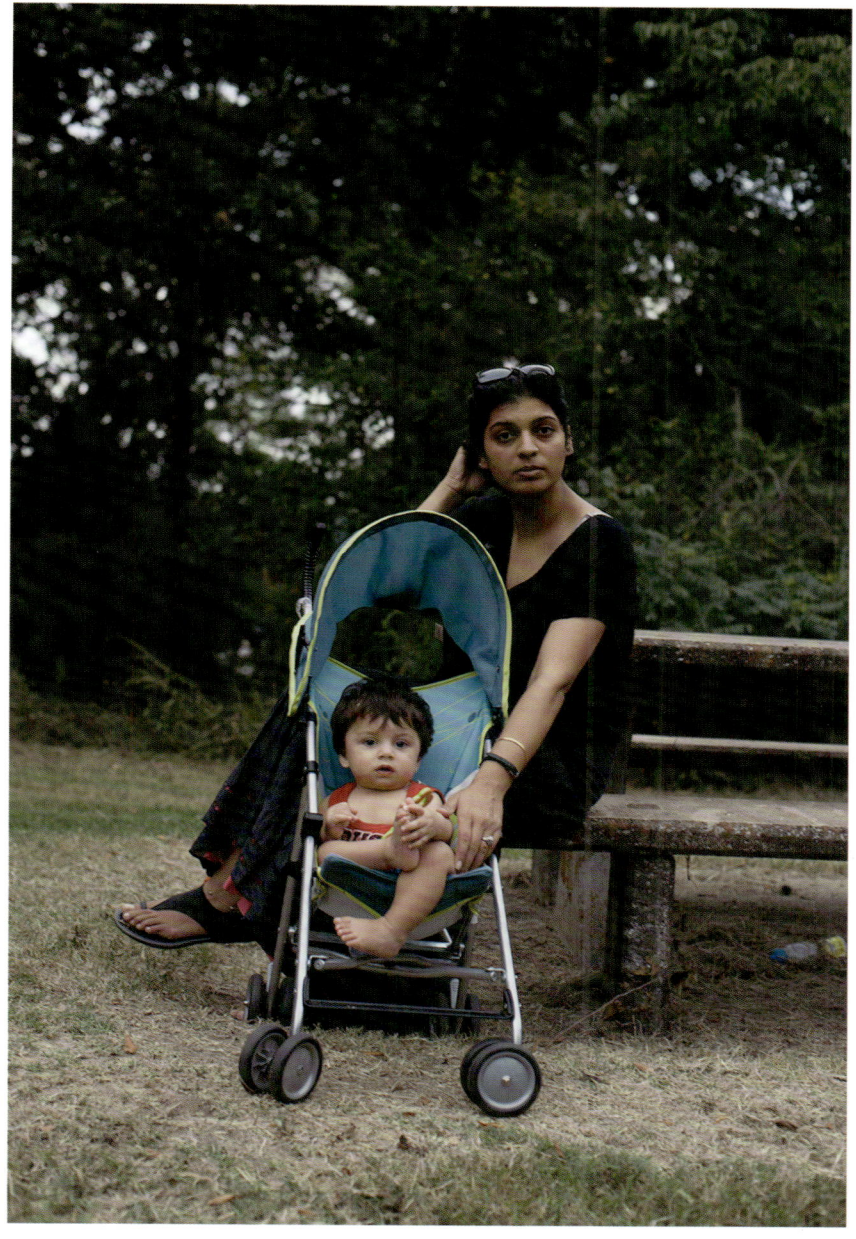

A new segment

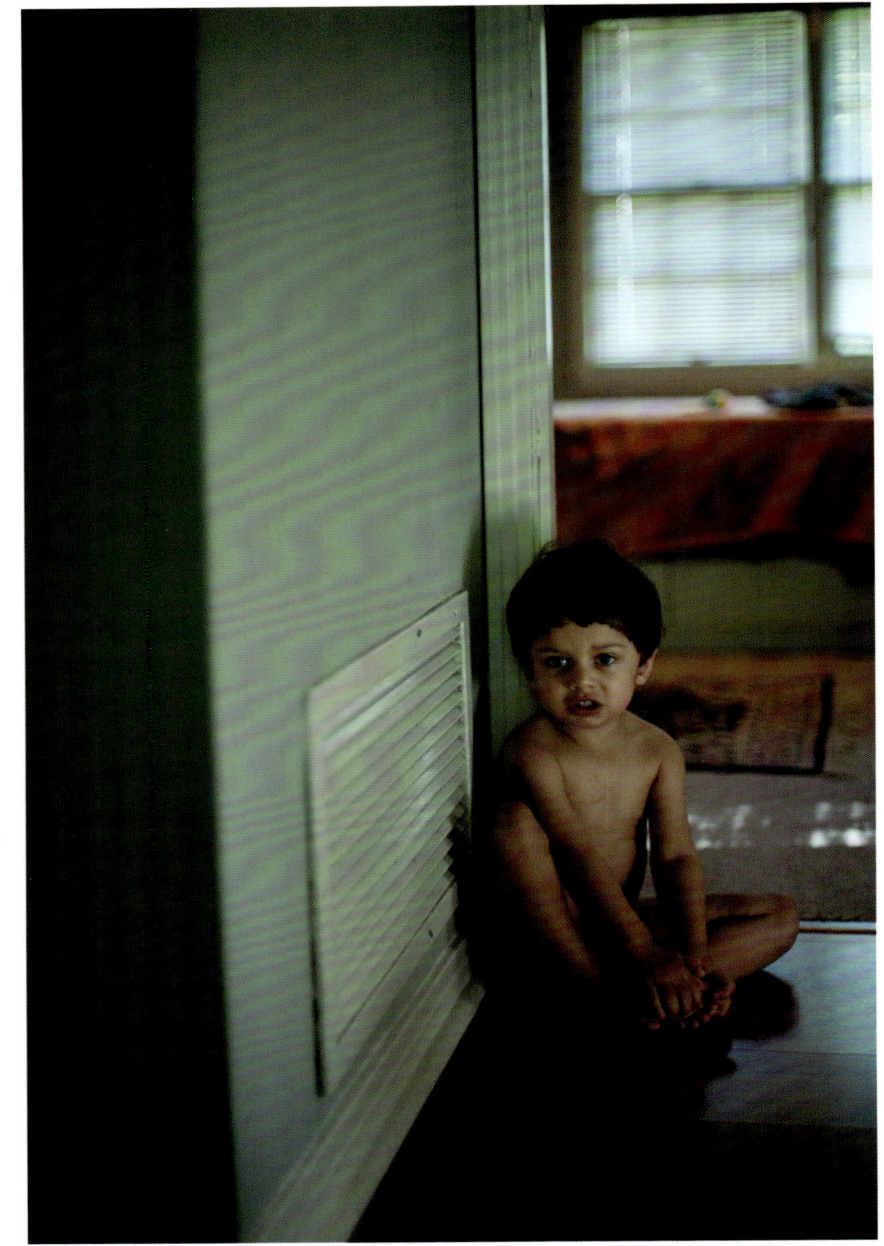

You stay frozen to the spot

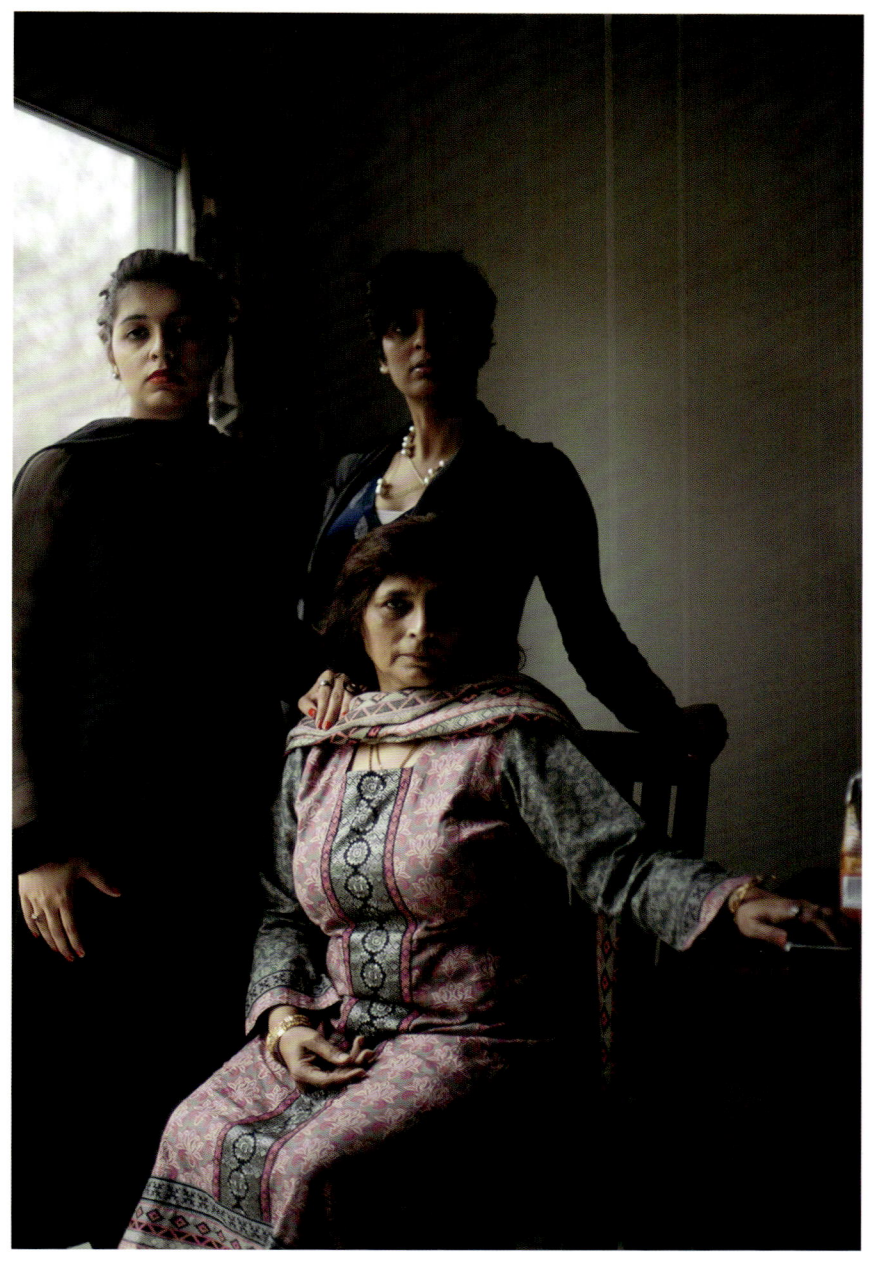

Neelam, Mehreen & Saher

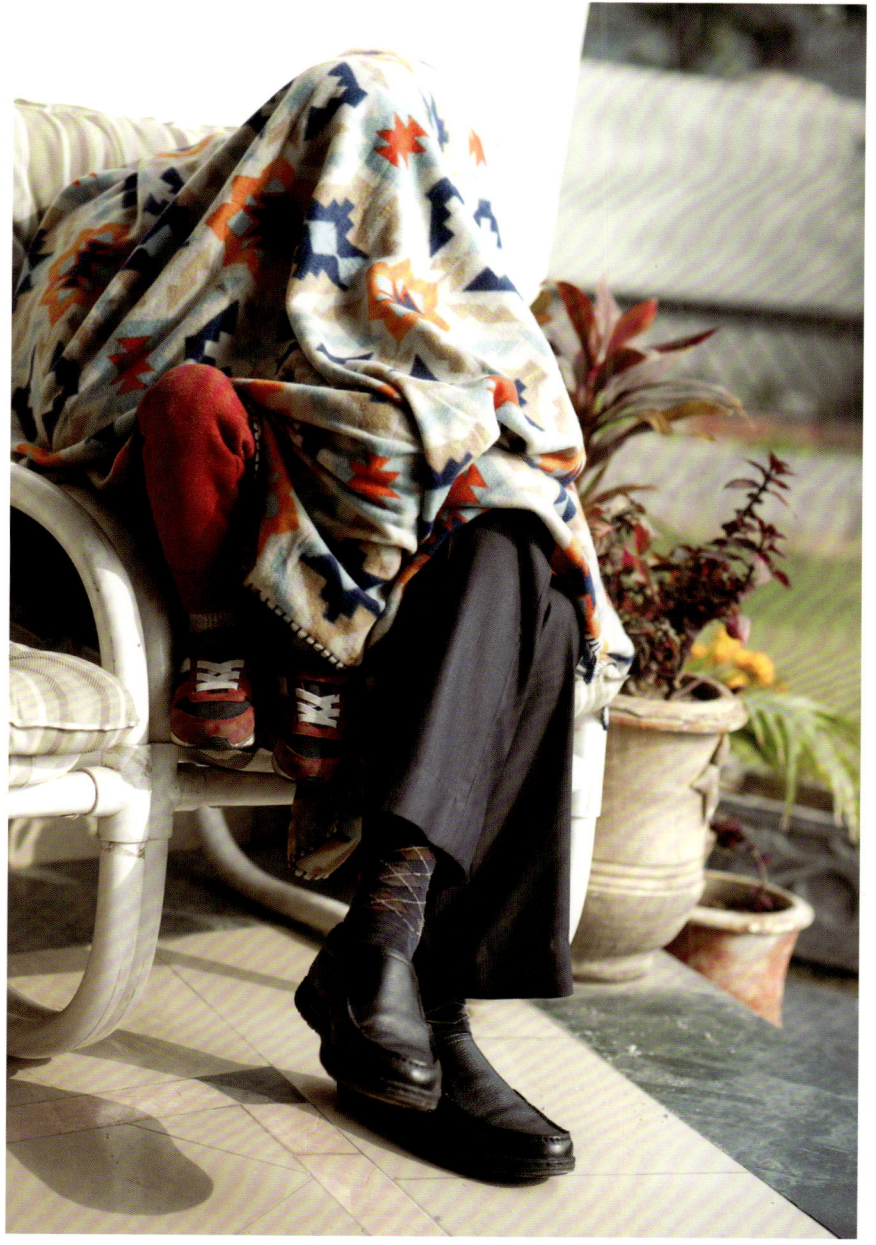

When the smog lifts up

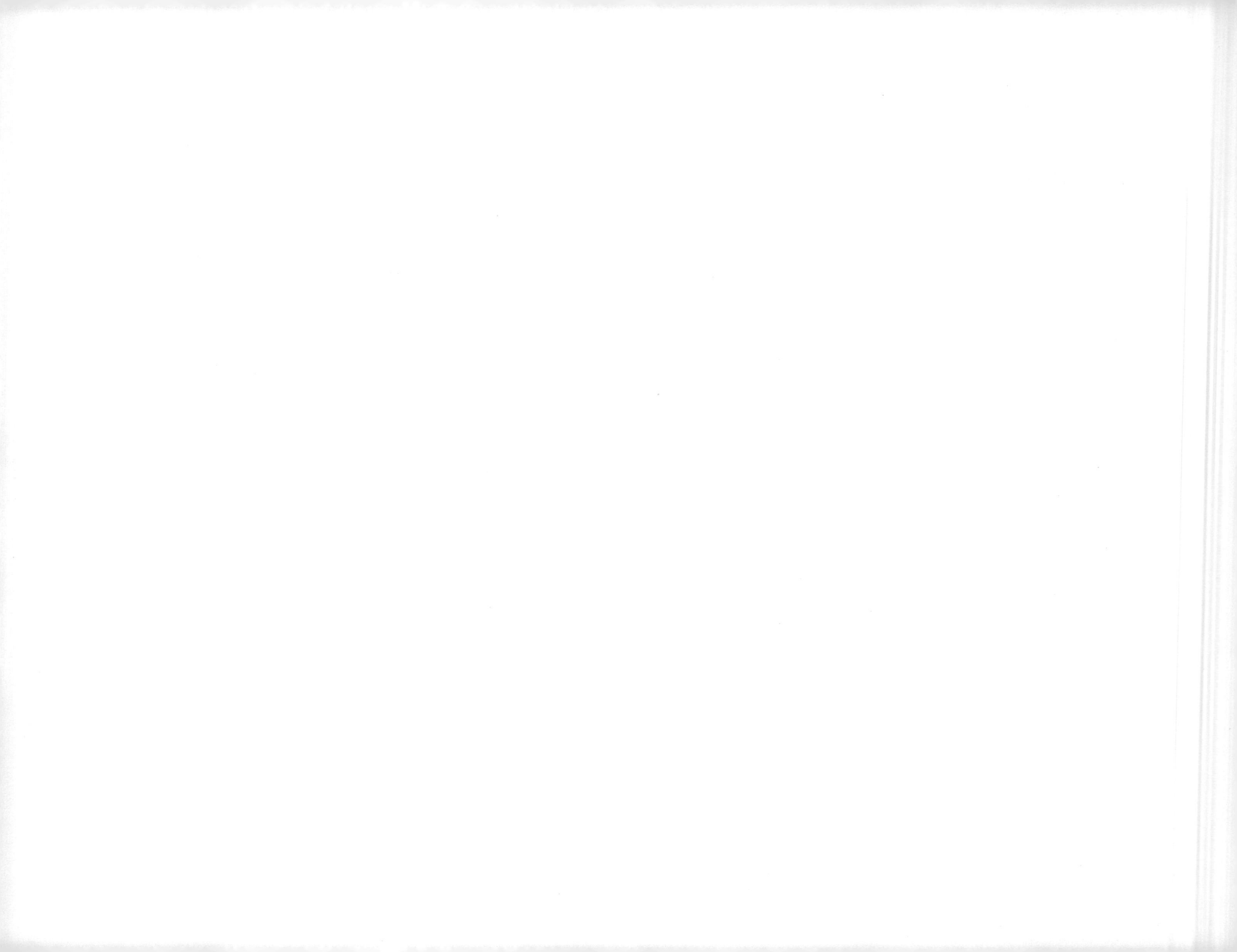

CHAPTER II

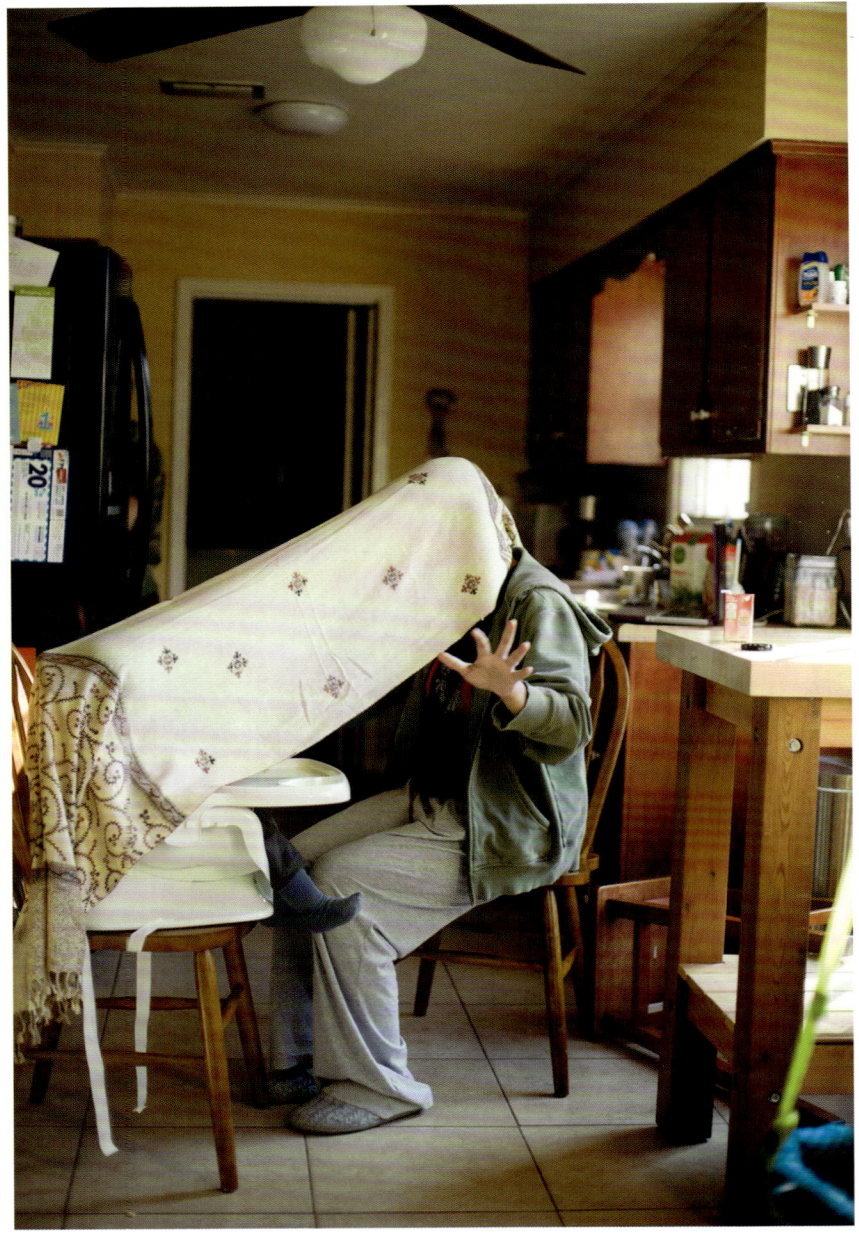

Bird in the window

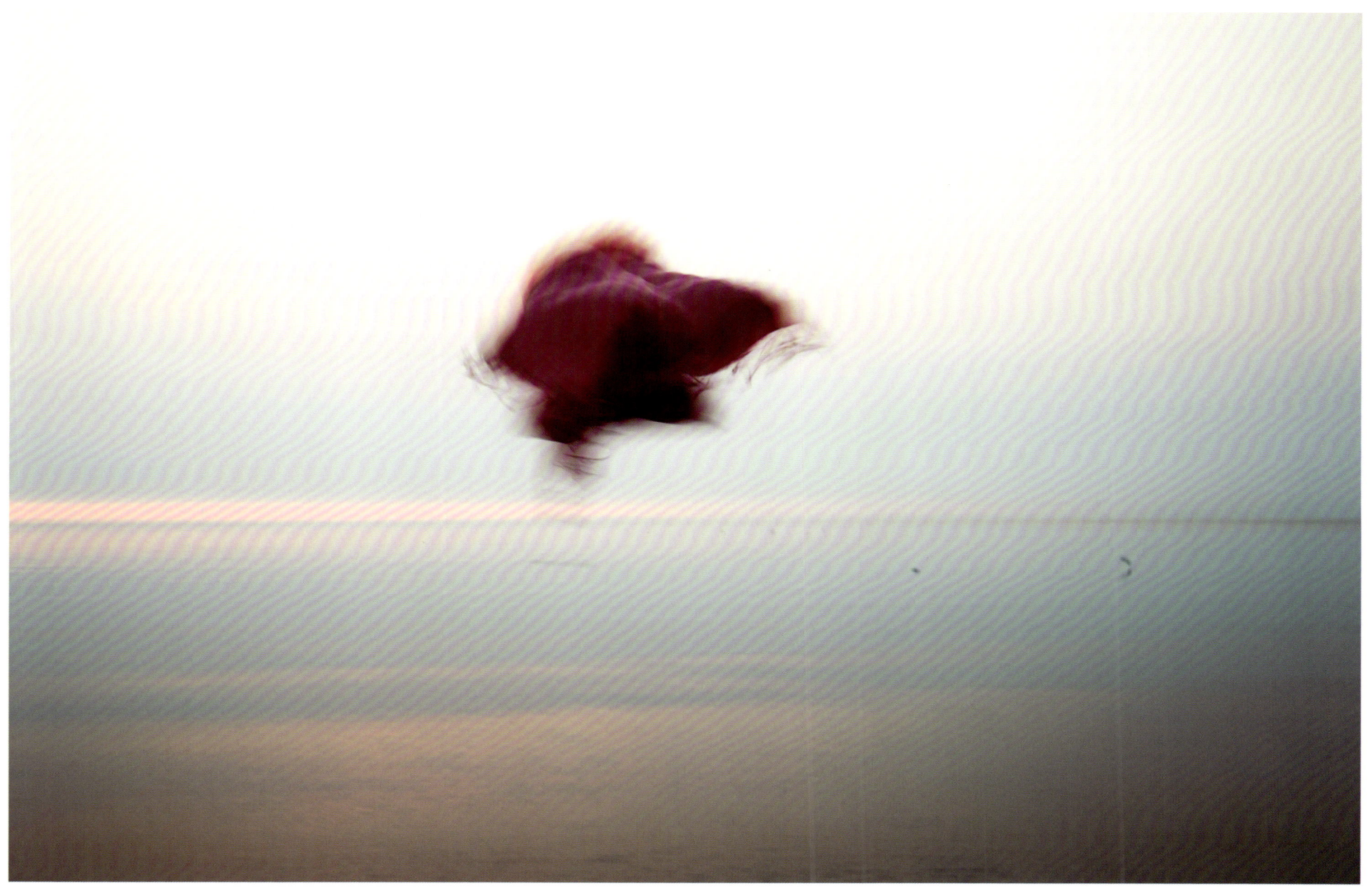

The high, recovering

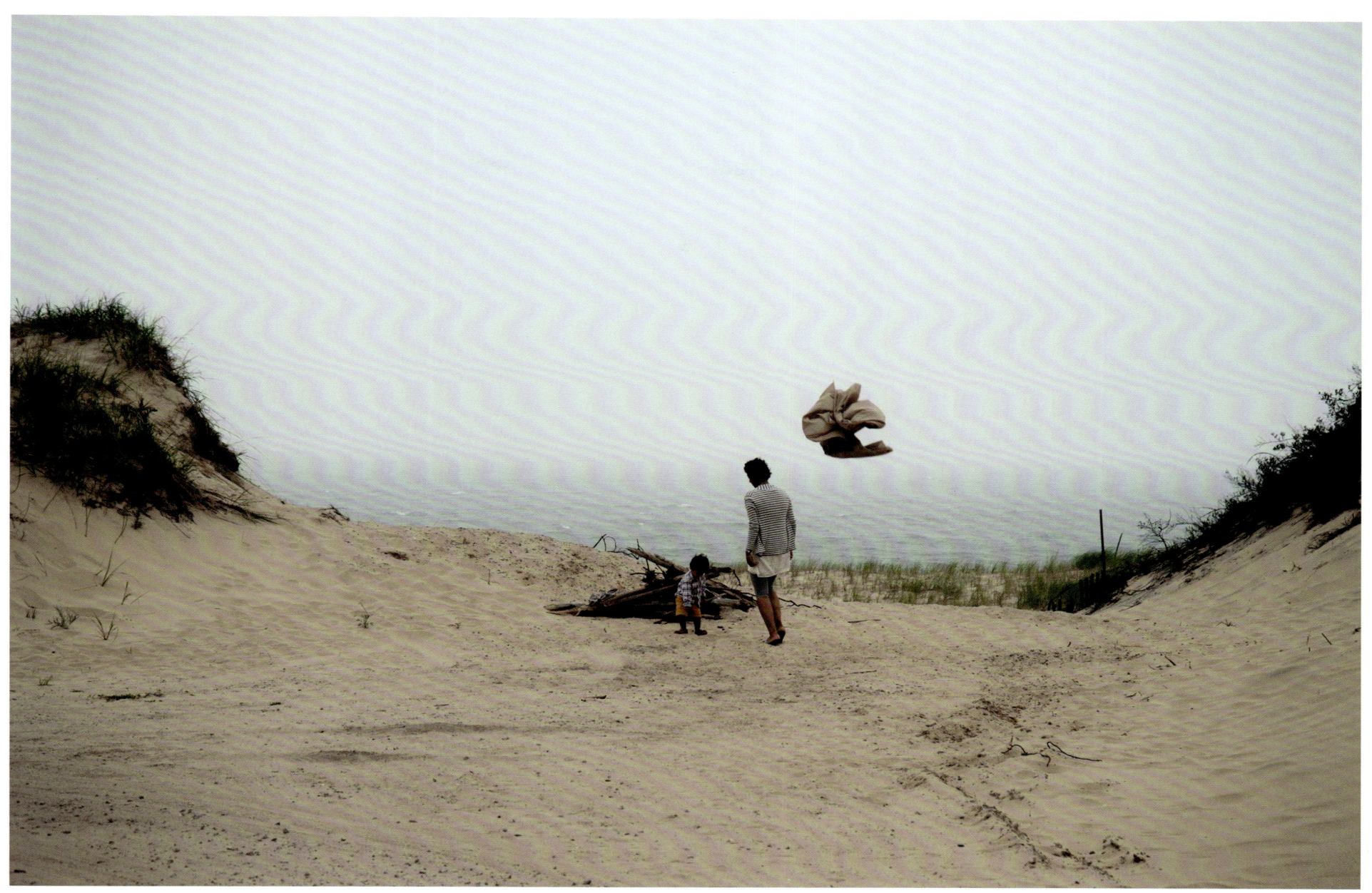

Because the fog came in

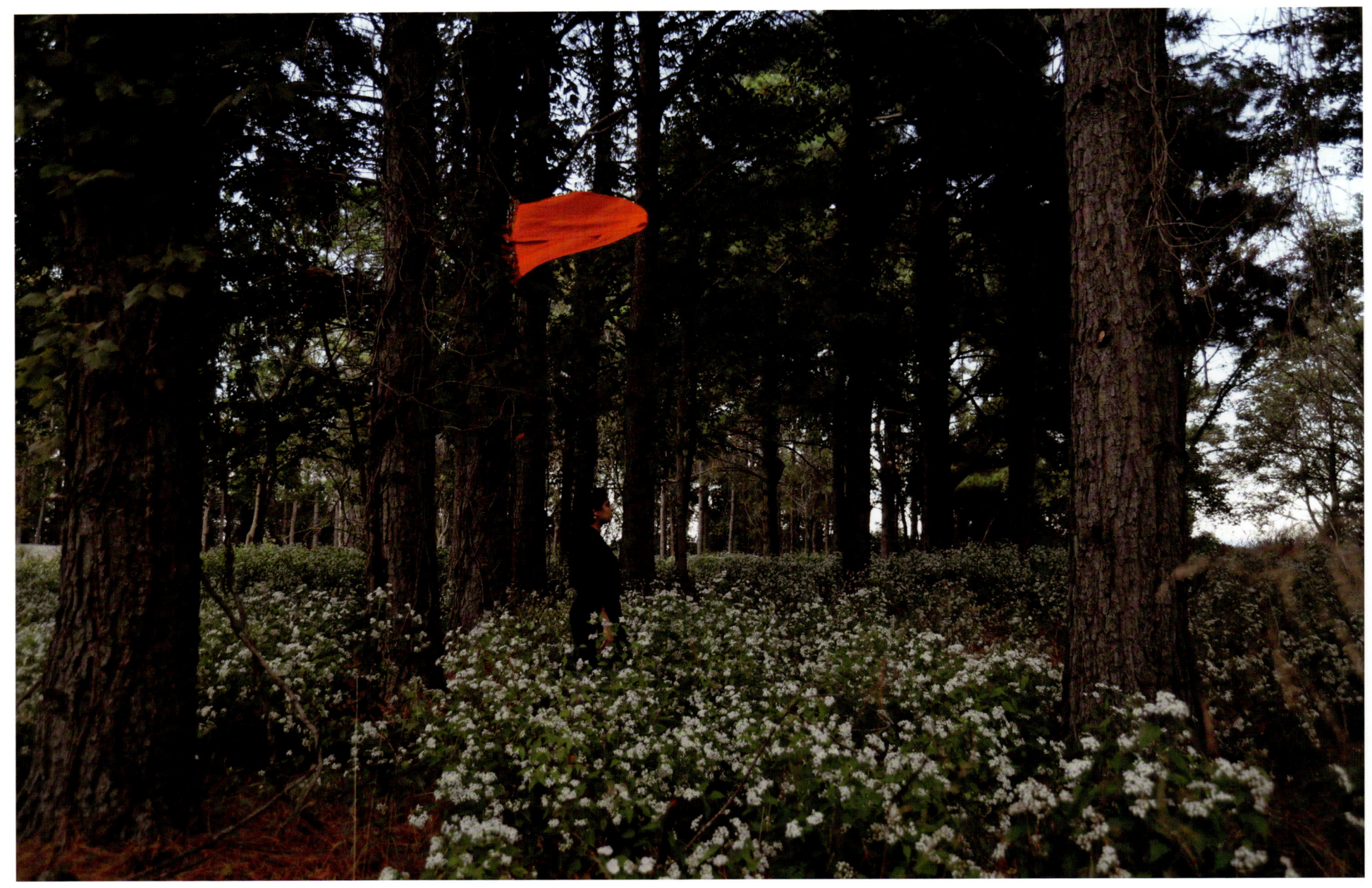

Facing south

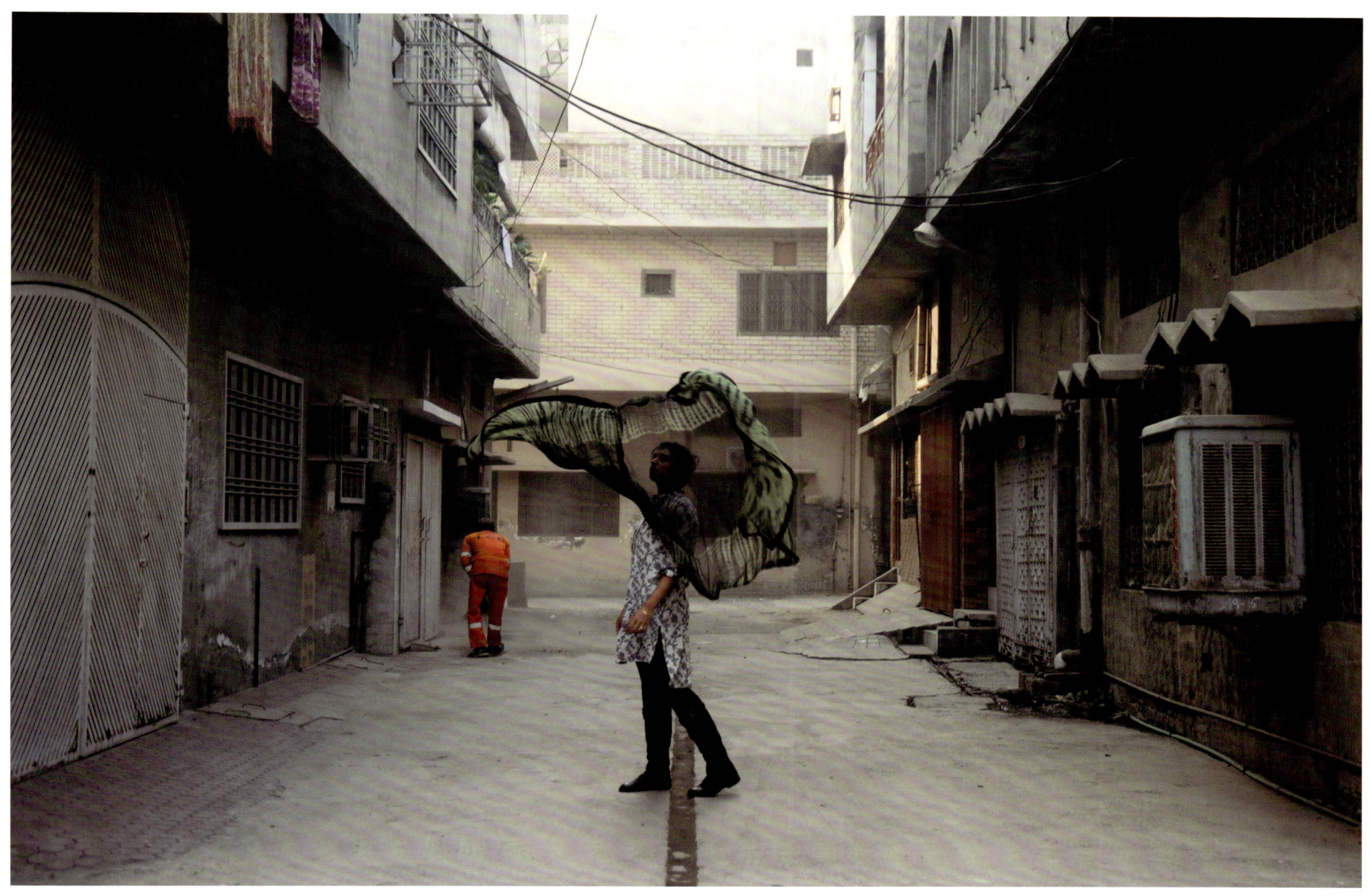

Narrow galian, tall houses

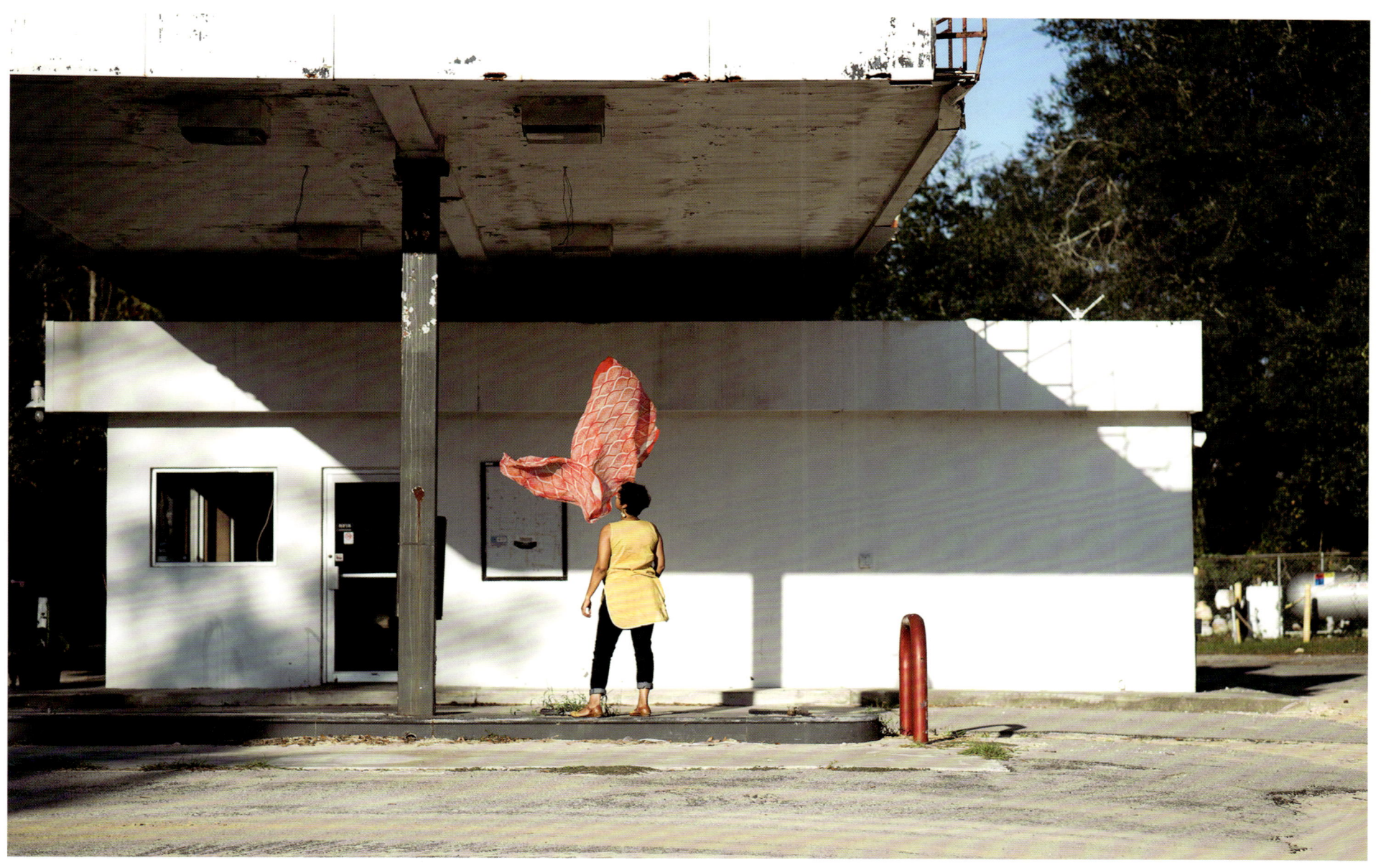

The escape, maybe it's near?

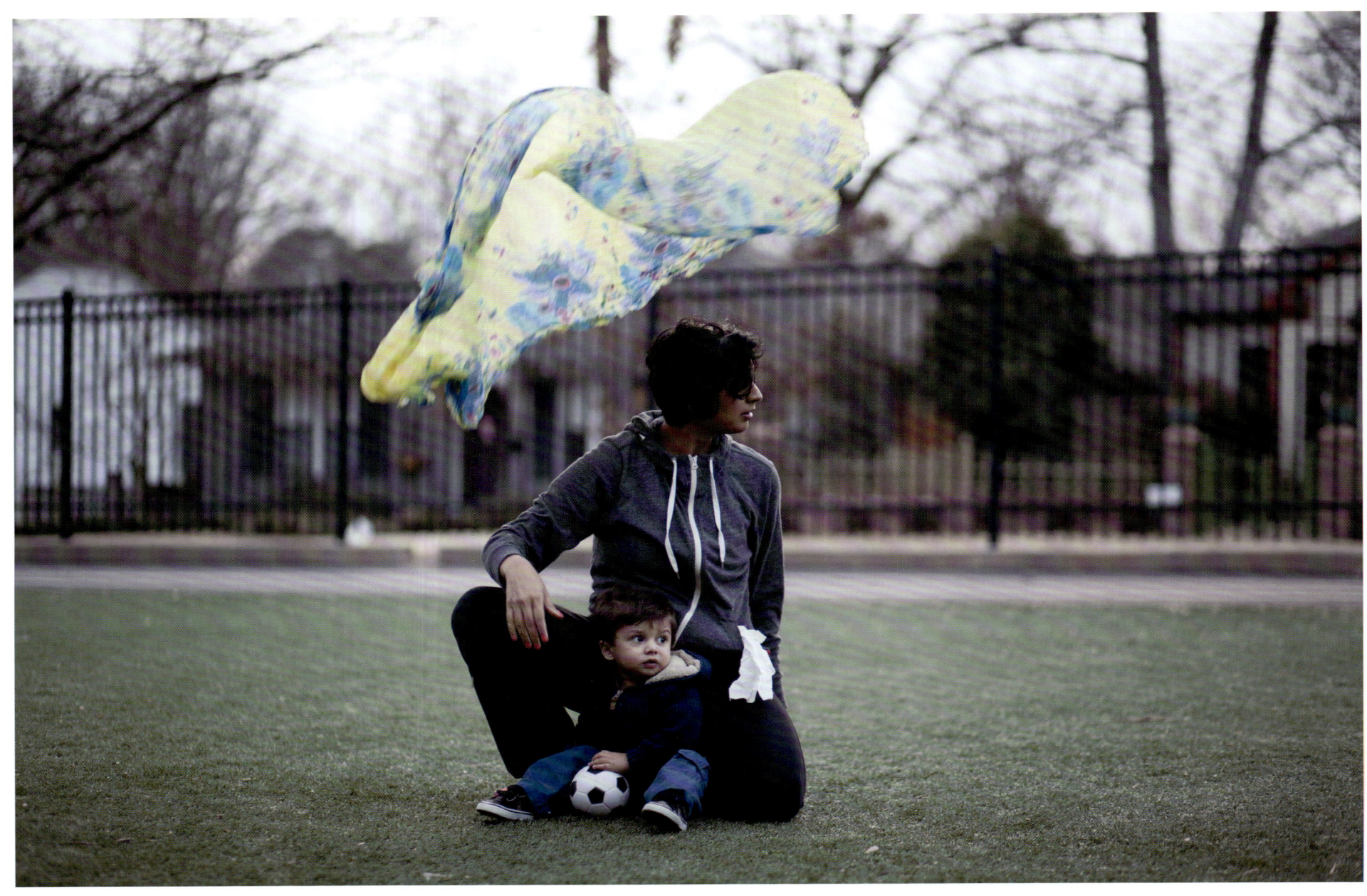

Those days, a memory

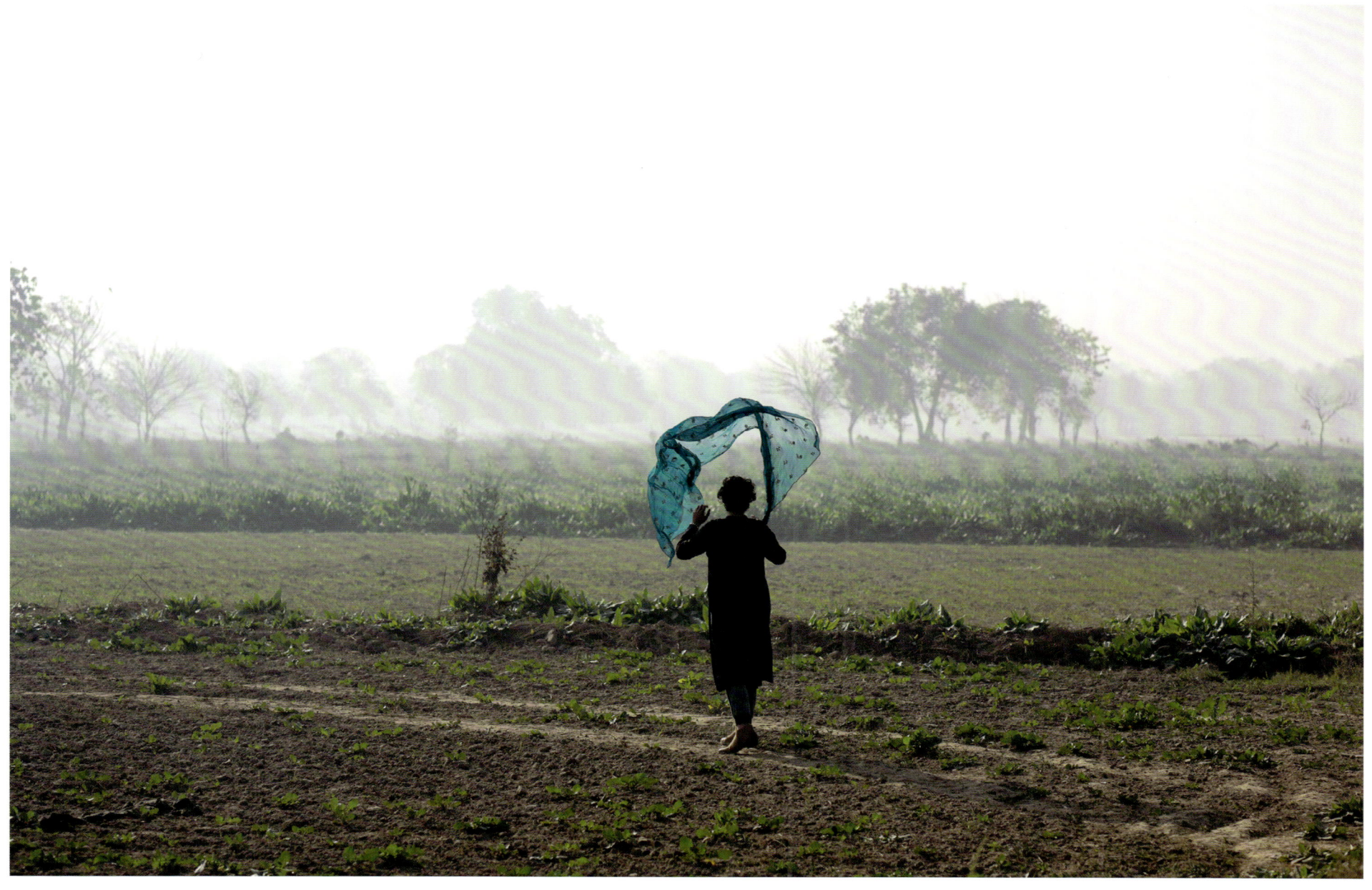

As the kites circled

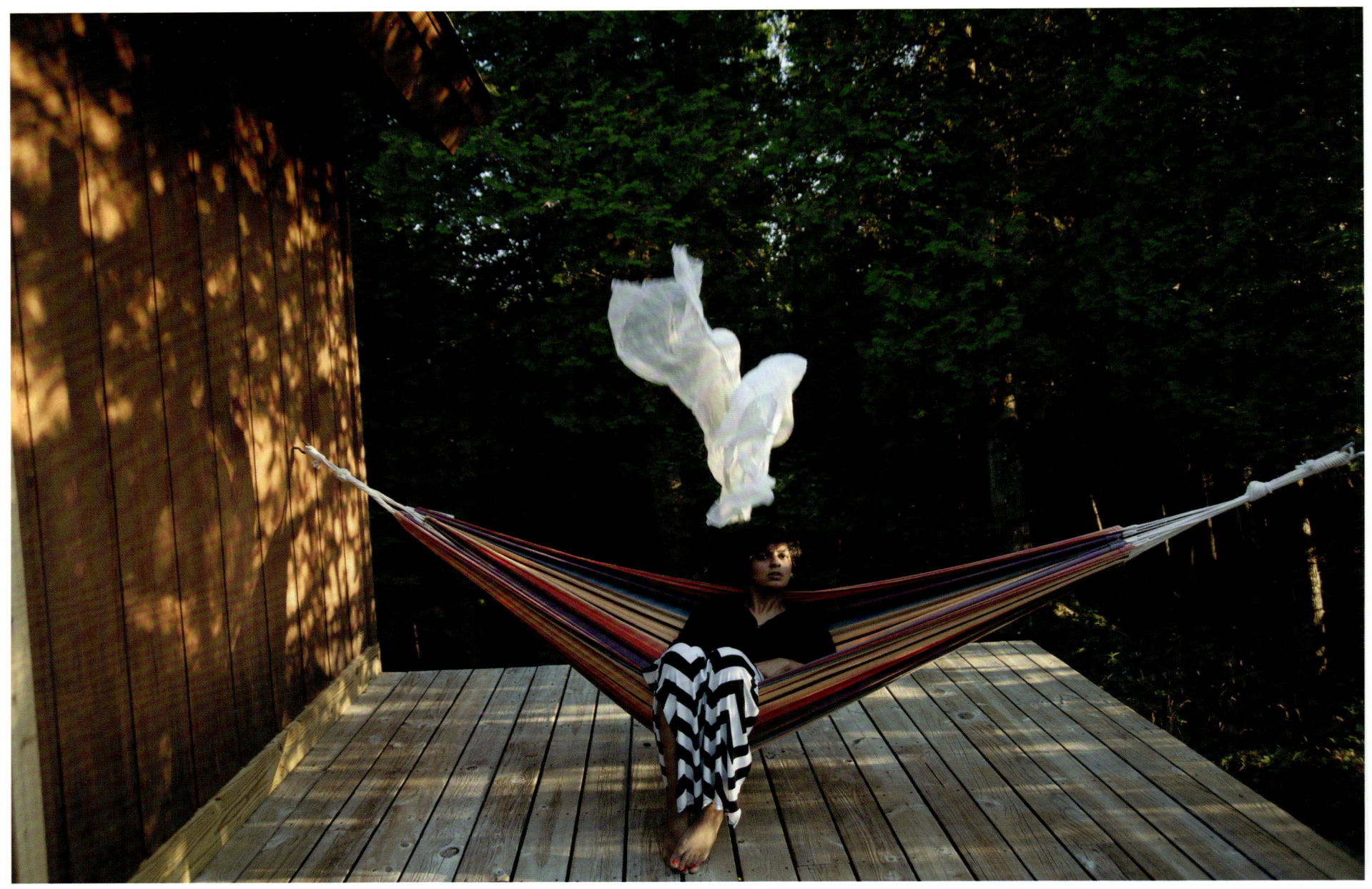

Of hammocks and sundials

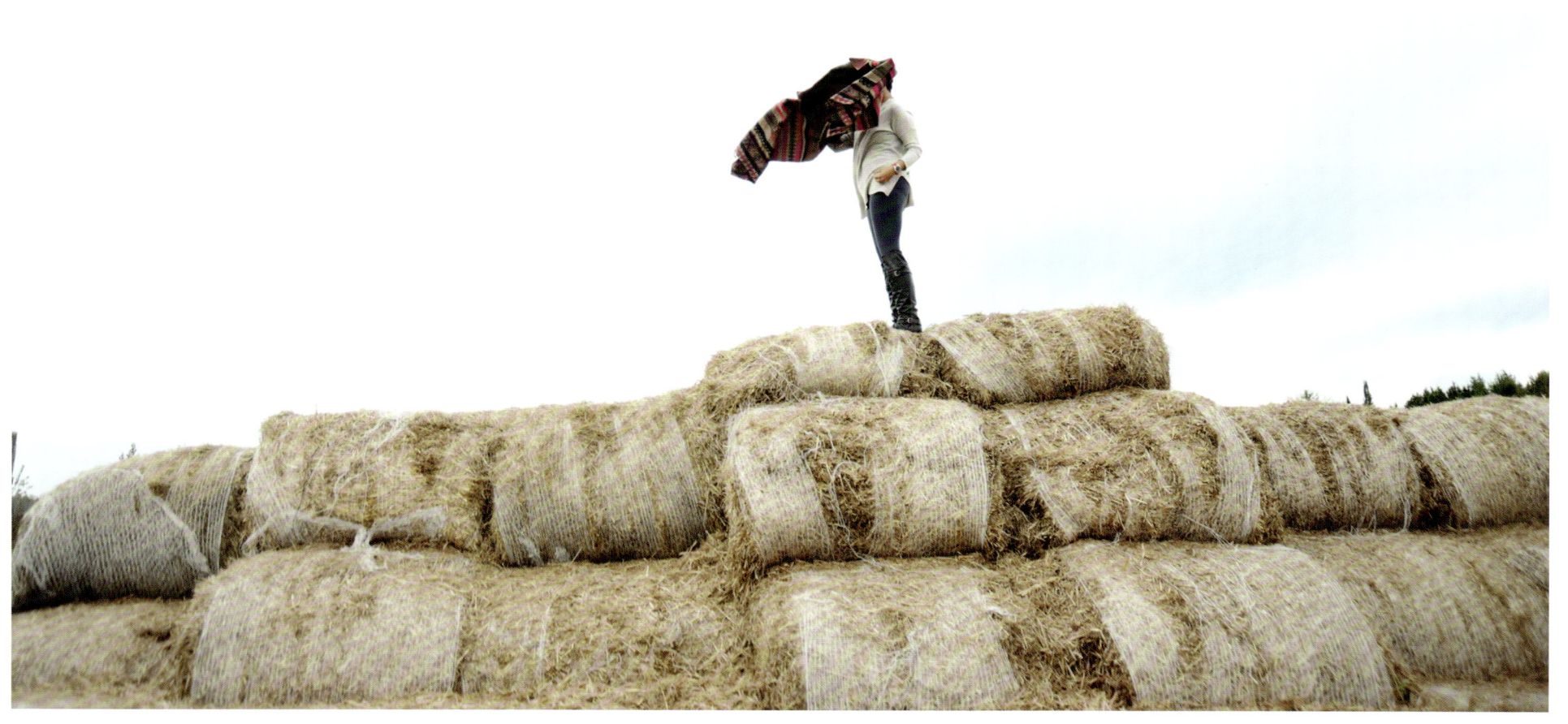

Standing still, as still as I can (remember?)

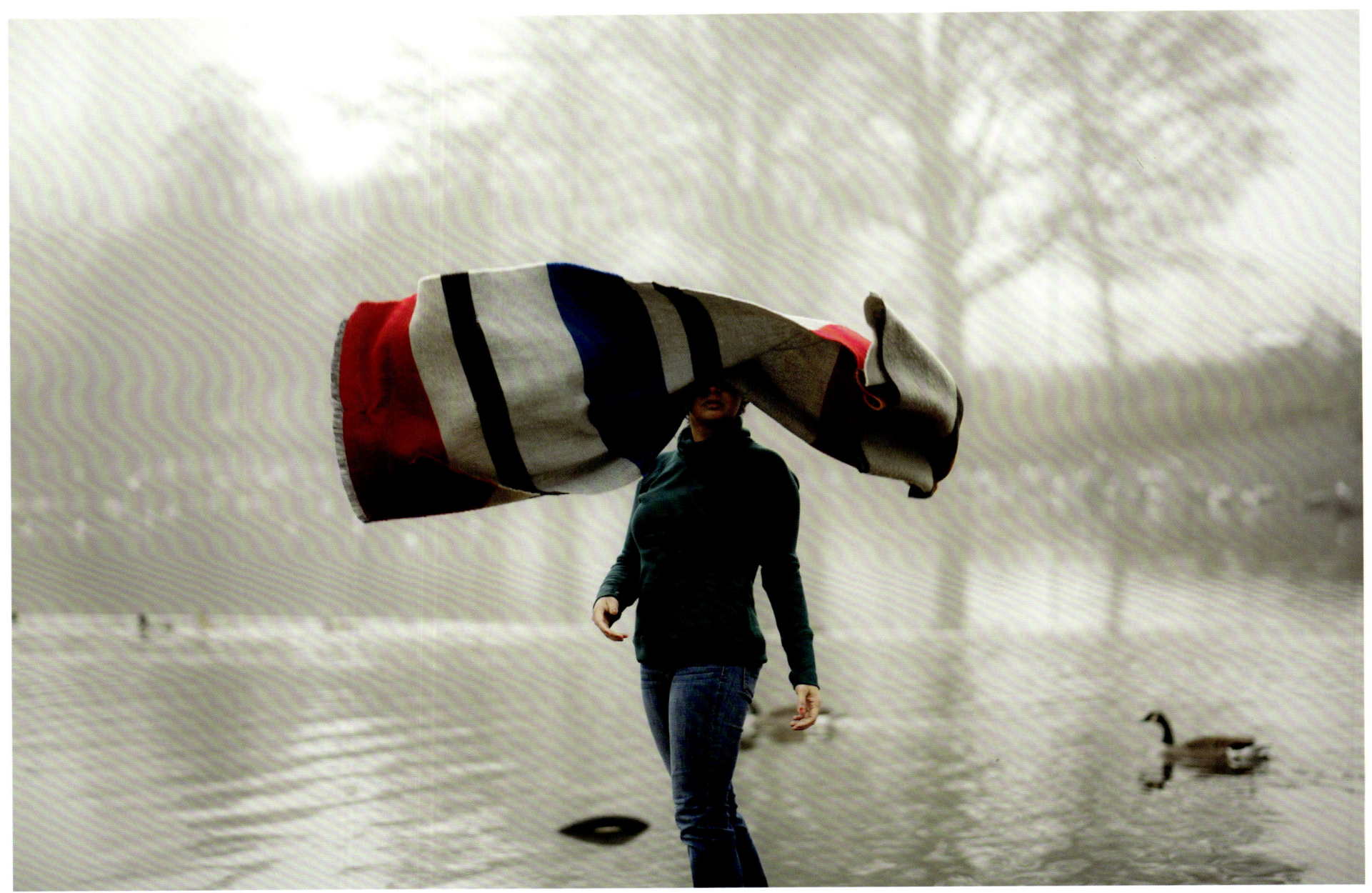

Dead fish, floating

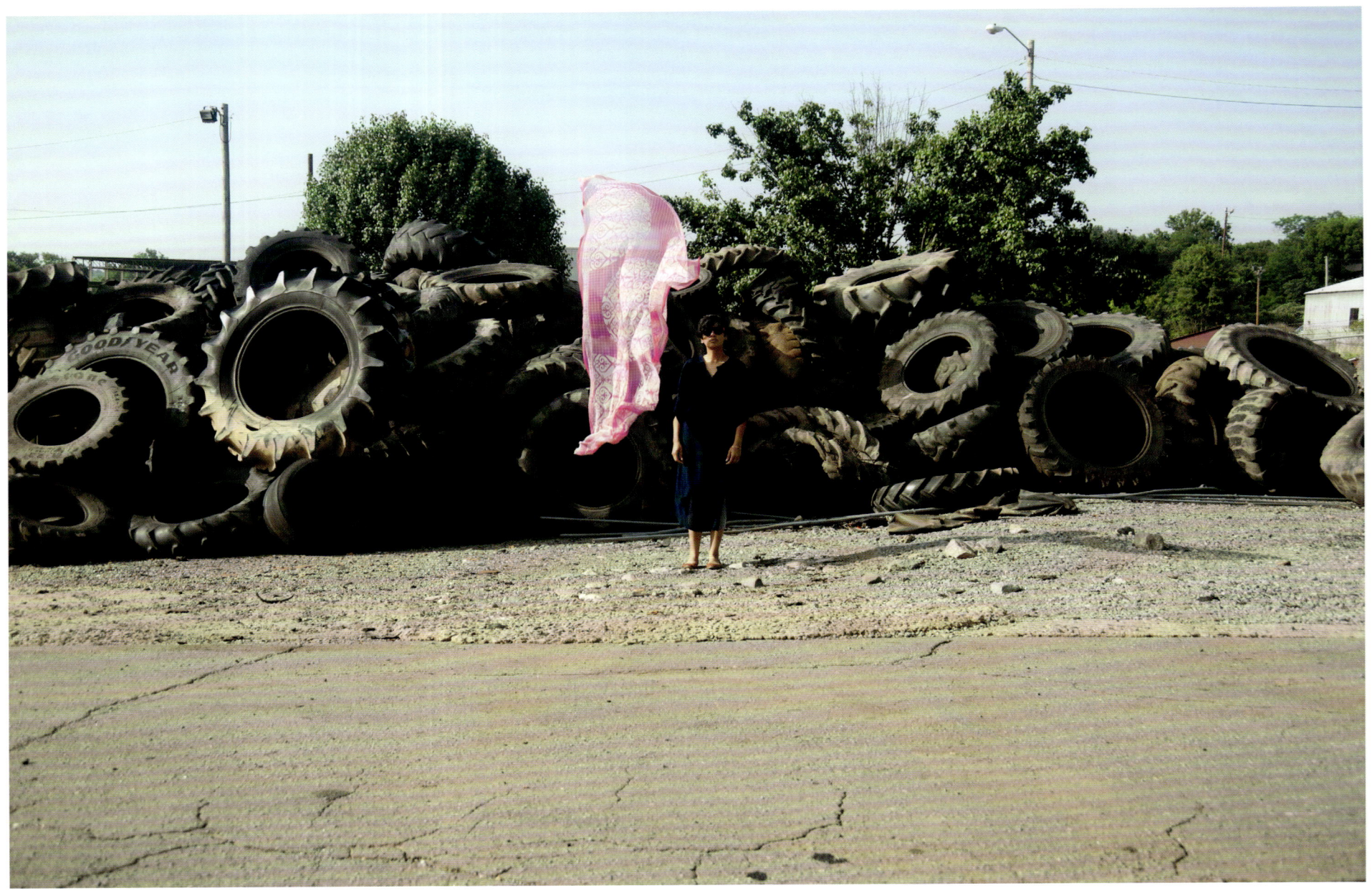

Of, home

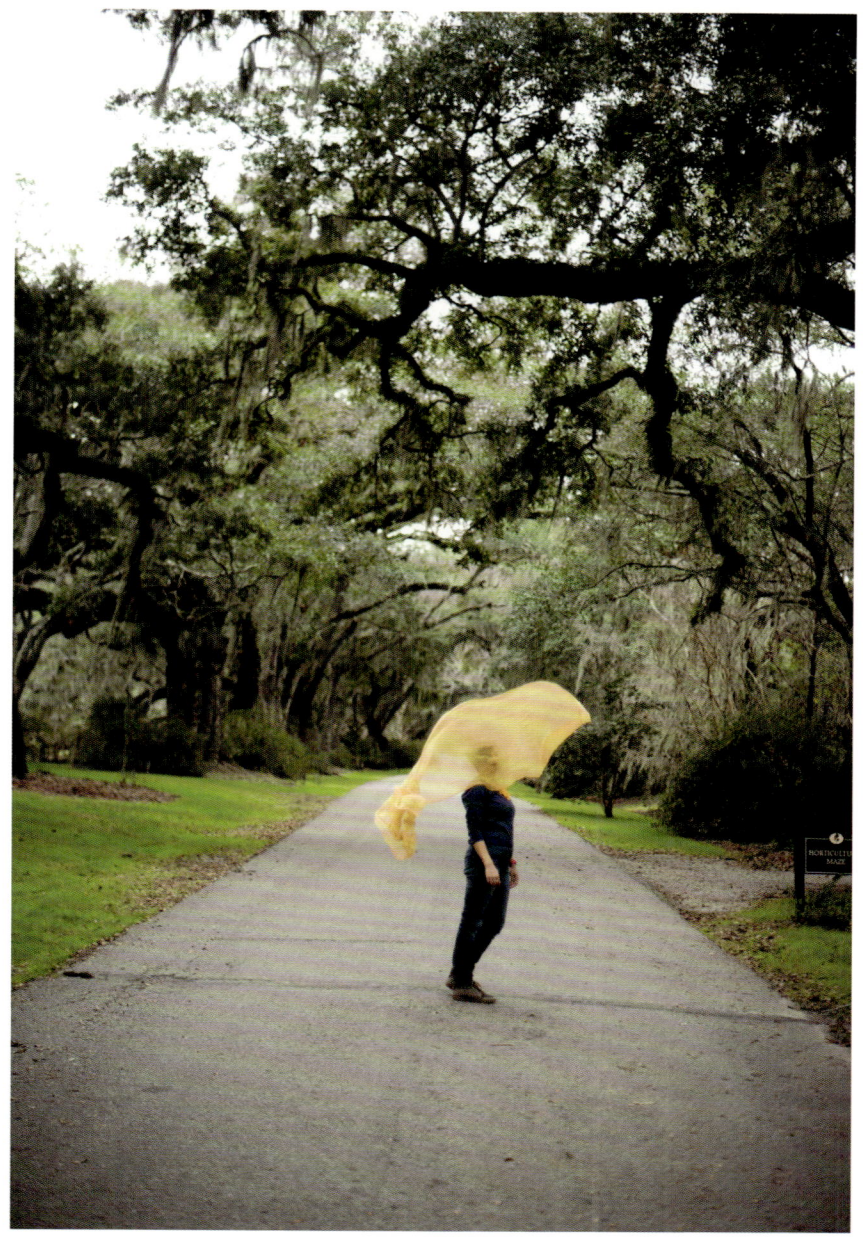

With Amma, praying

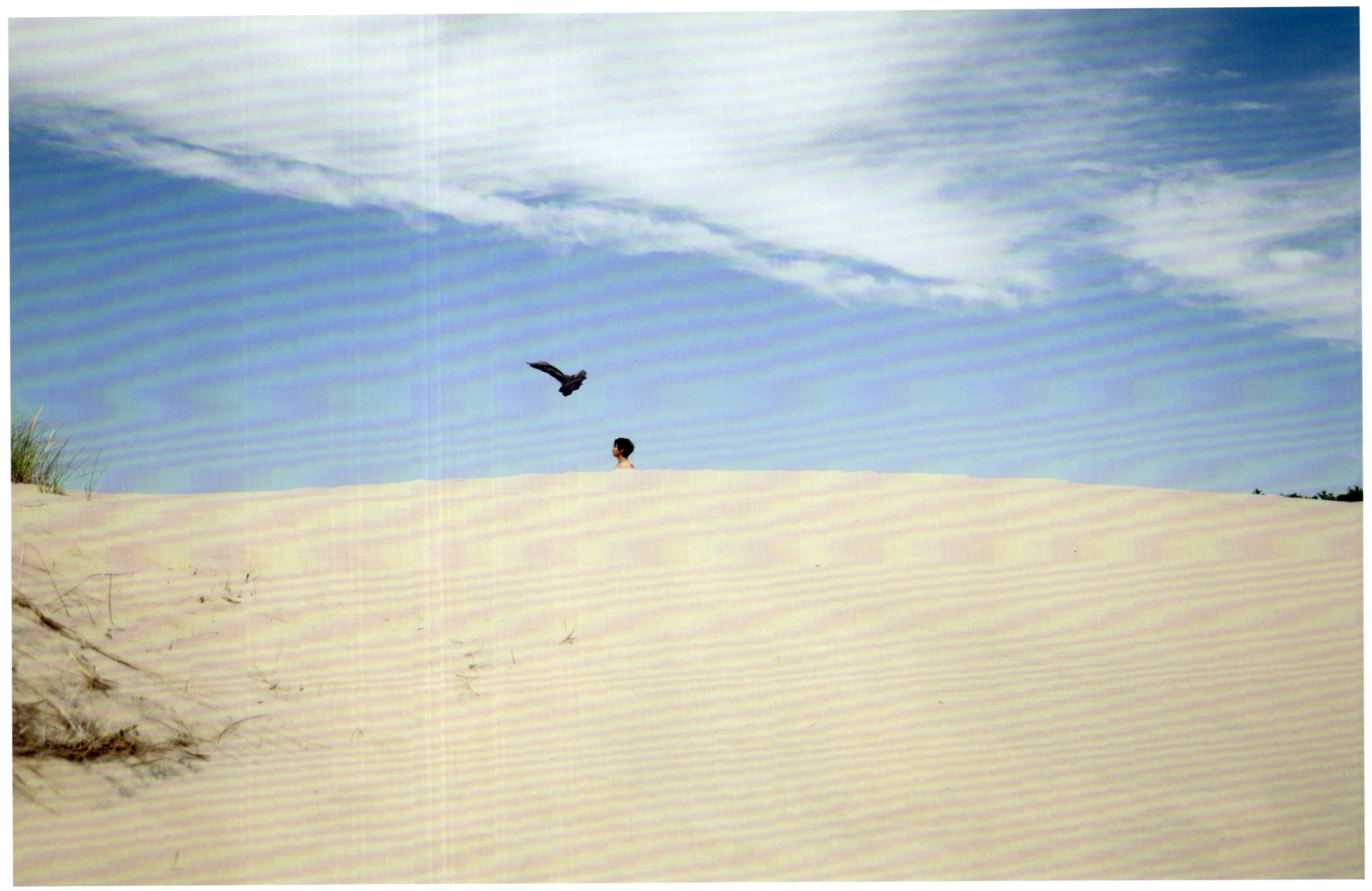

As I disappear

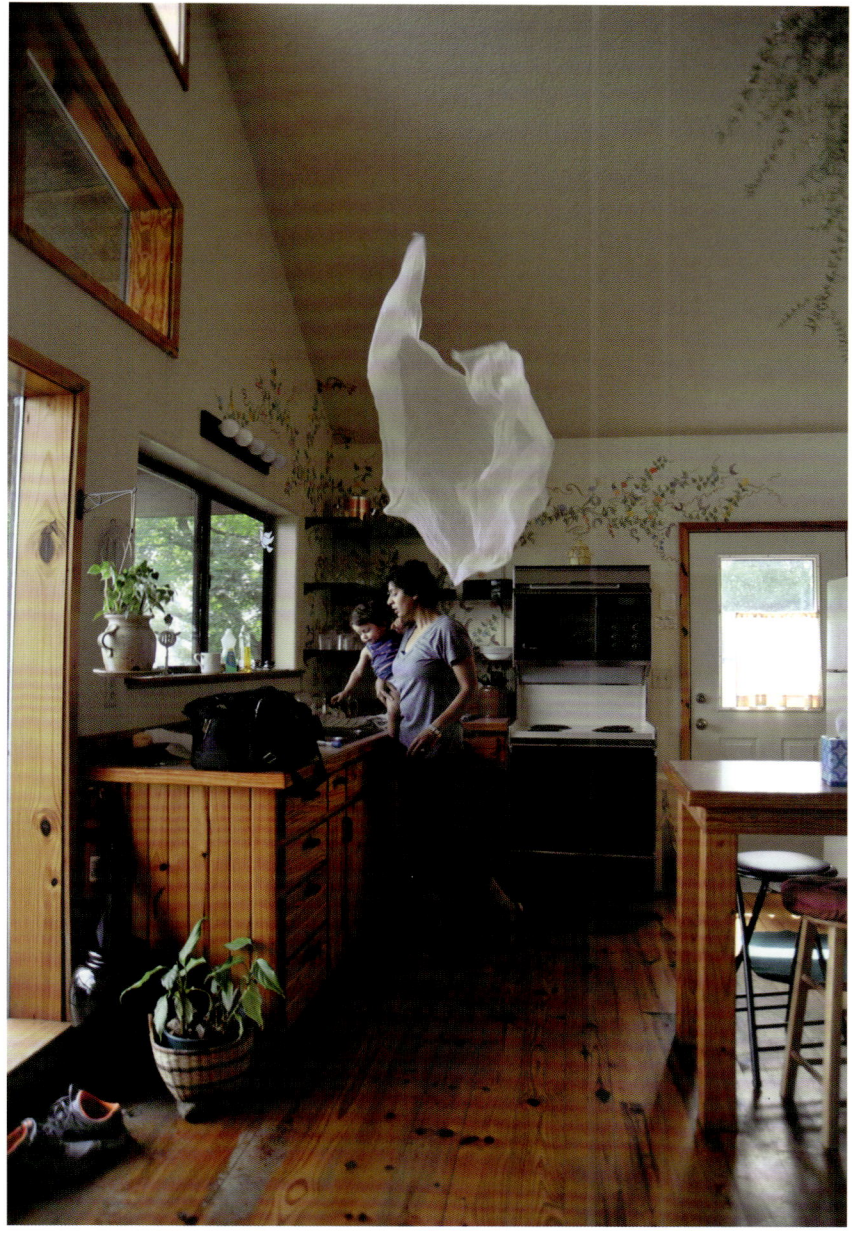

Seconds before leaving

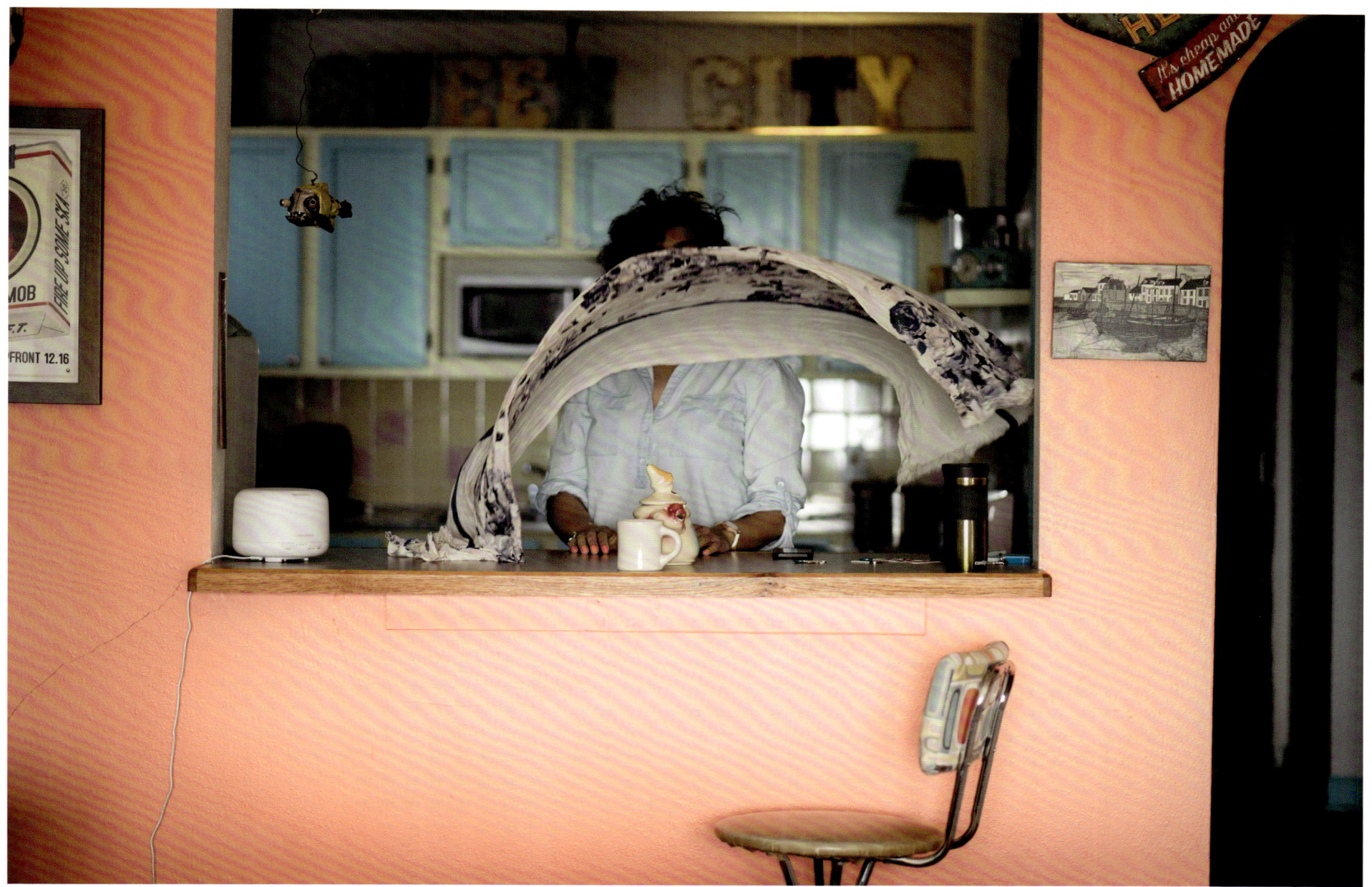

A new stage

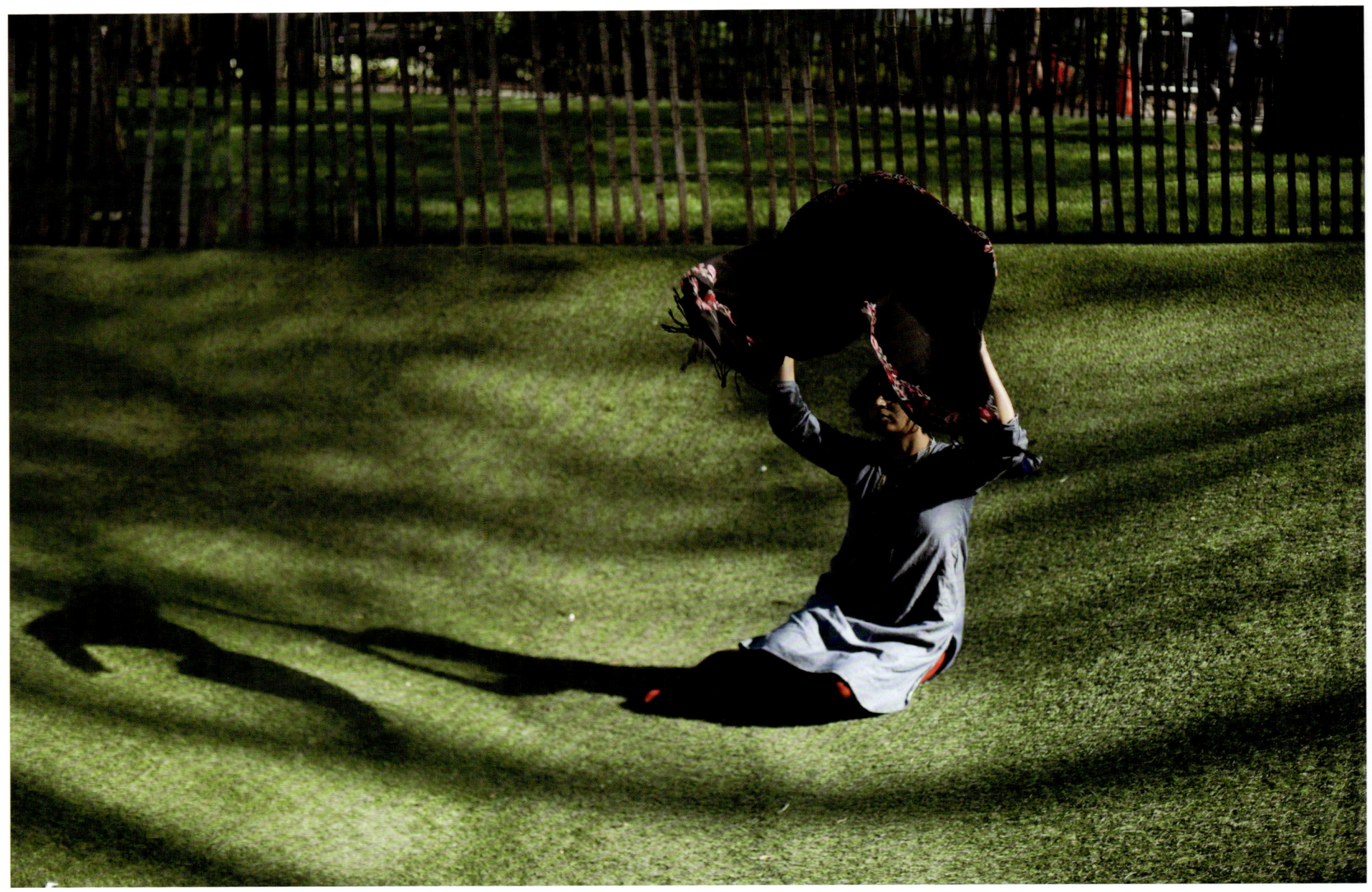

Before it collapsed

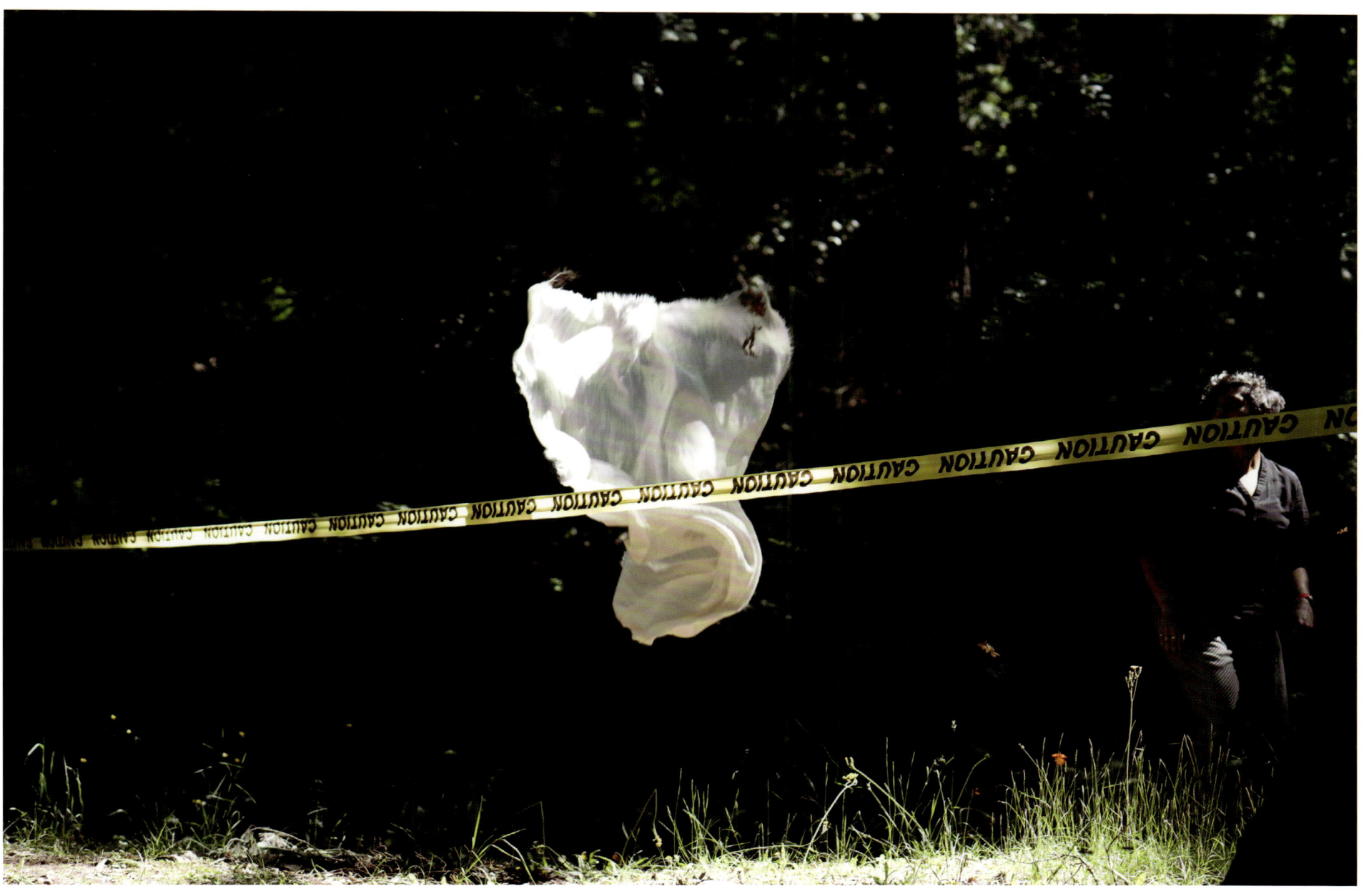

When are you coming back?

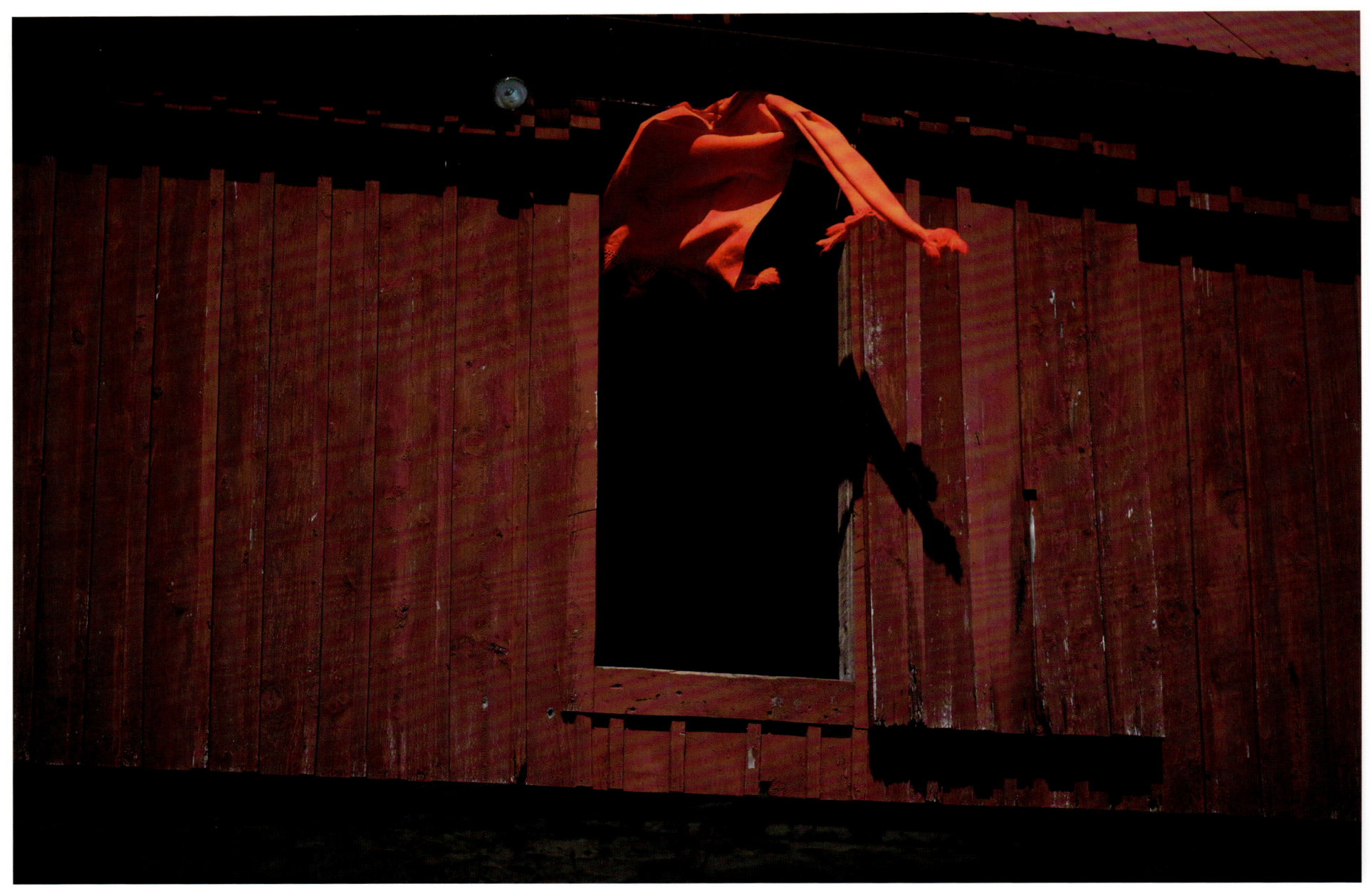

Weeded ponds and stone walls

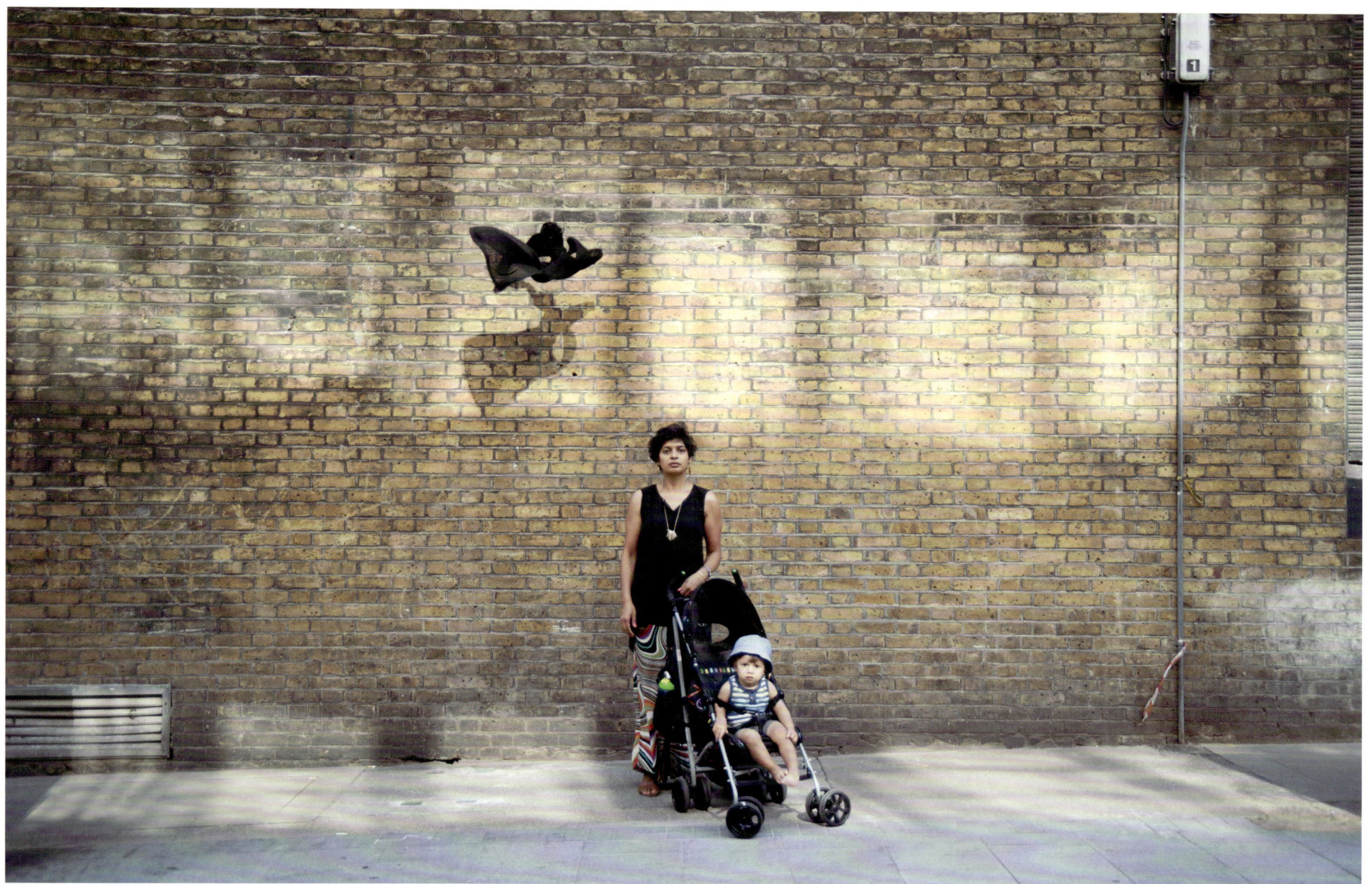

Pursuing the light

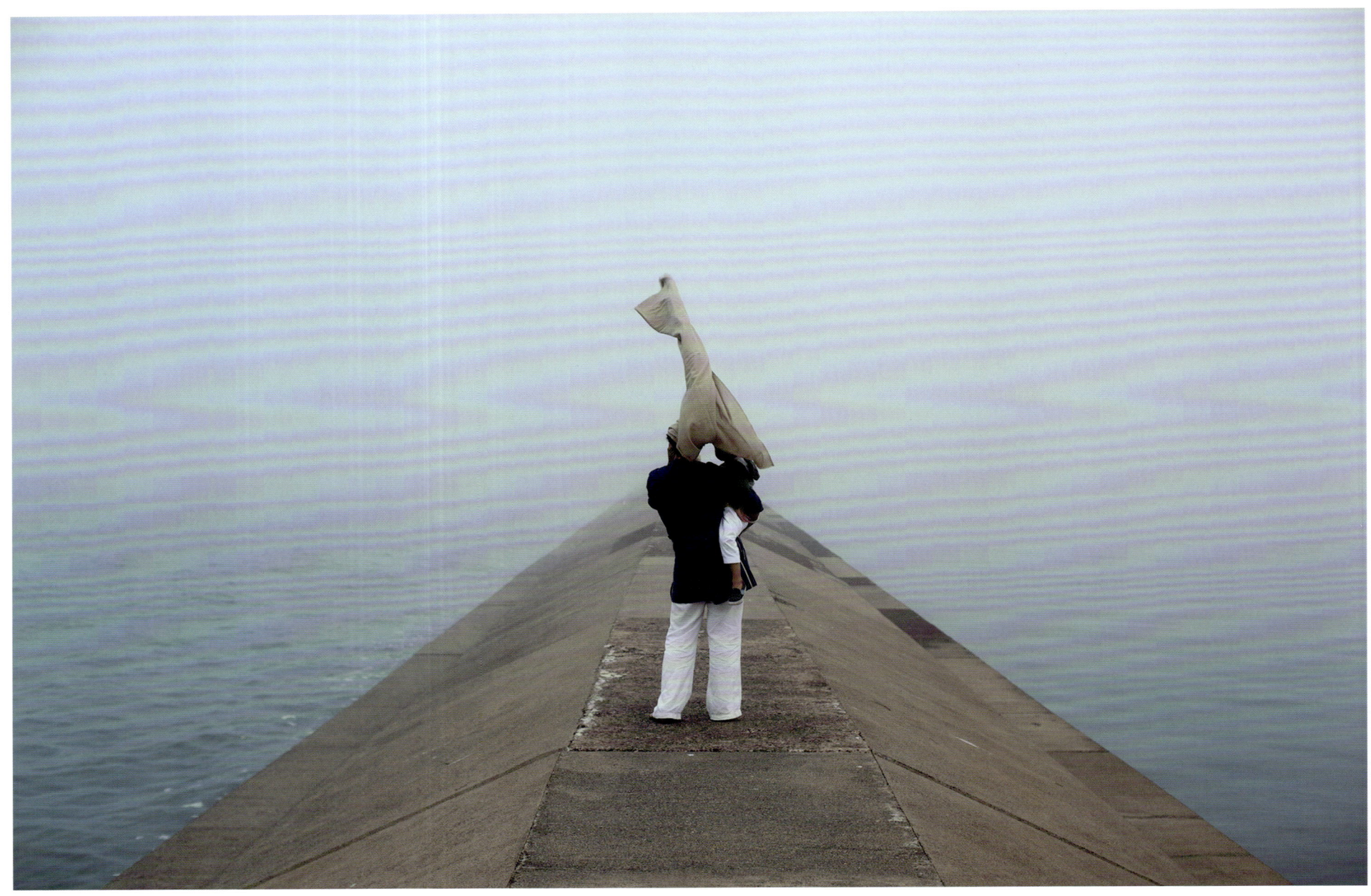

The last goodbye

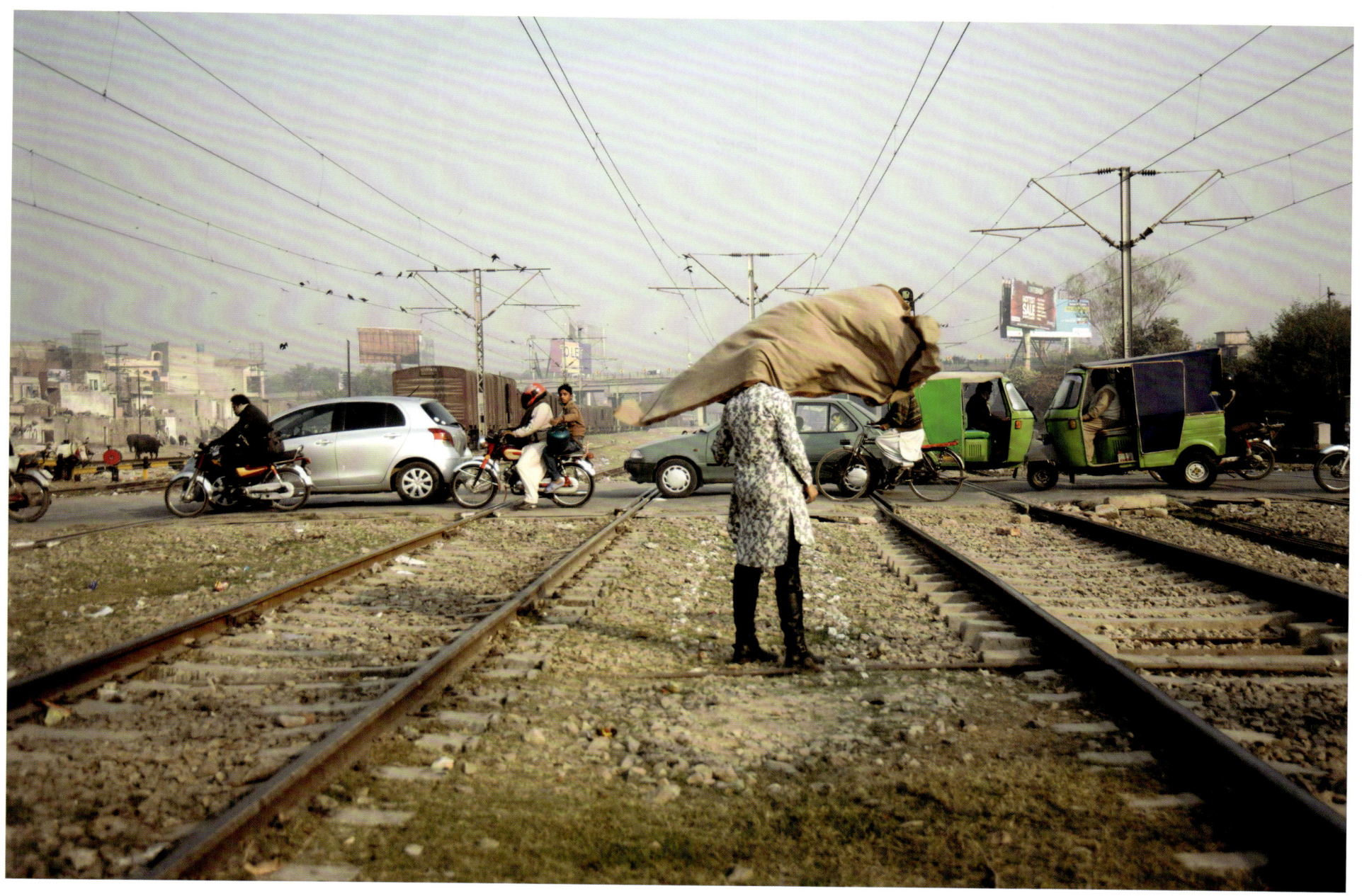

Watching me, watching you

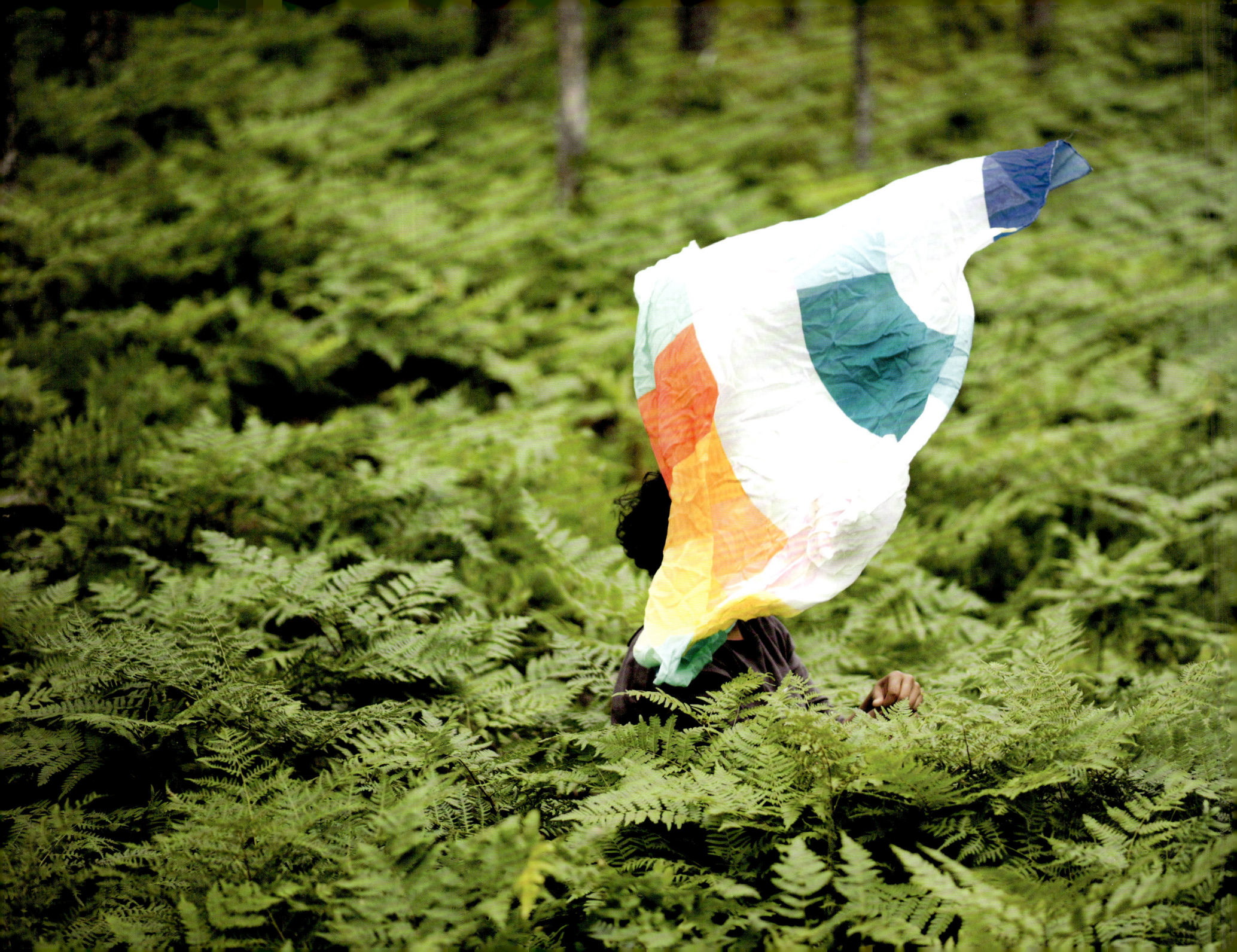

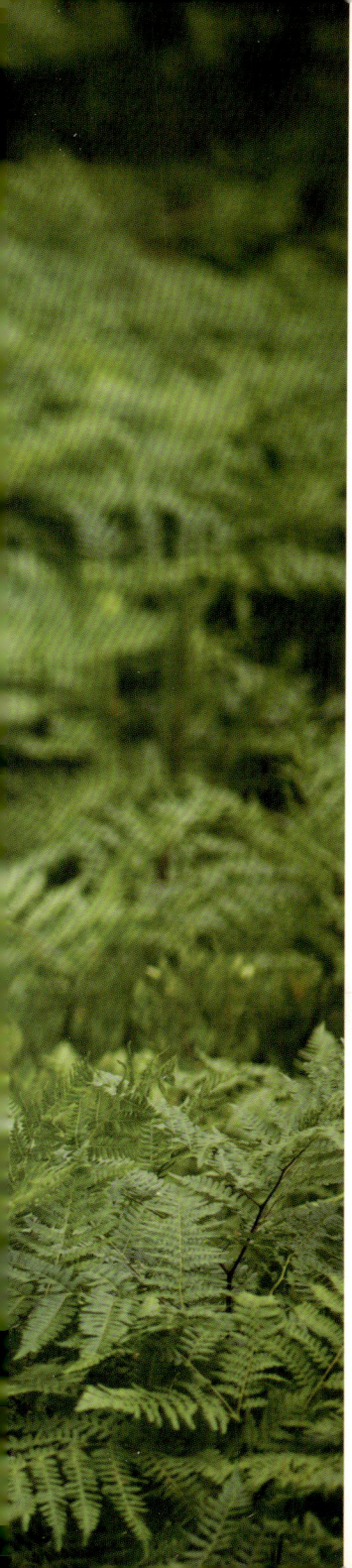

First, maybe the last?

CHAPTER III

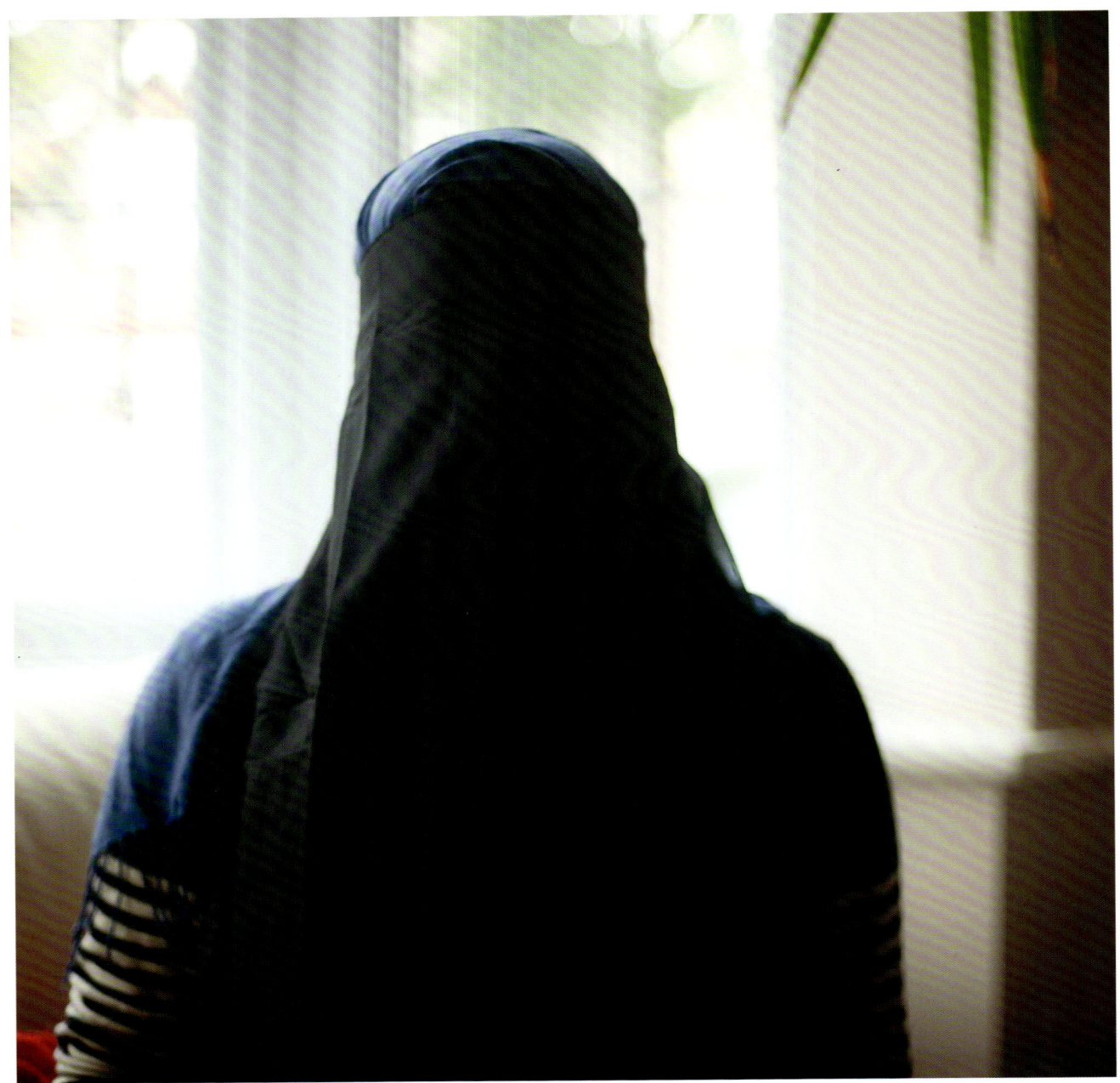

While they waited

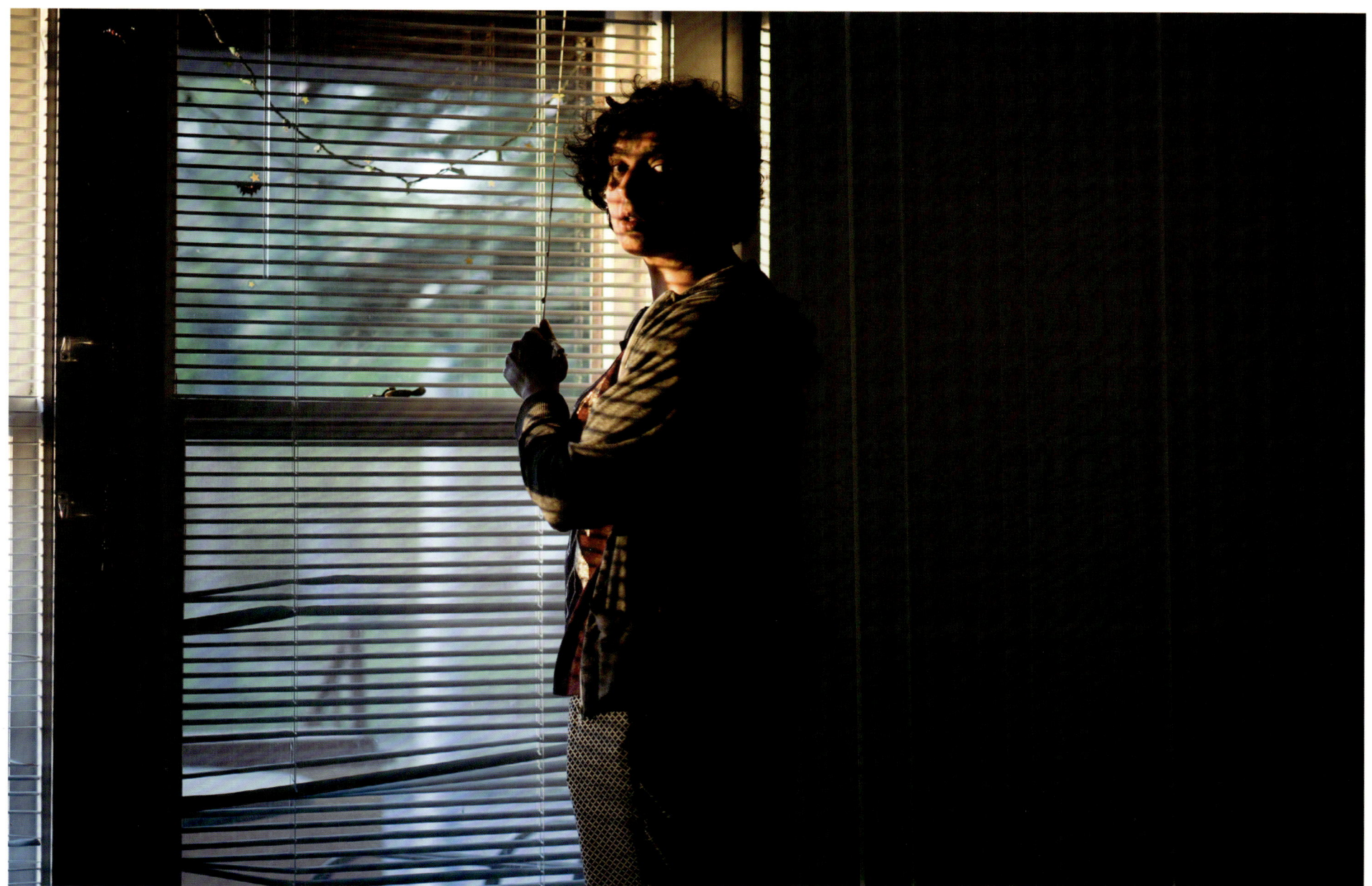

Before darkness

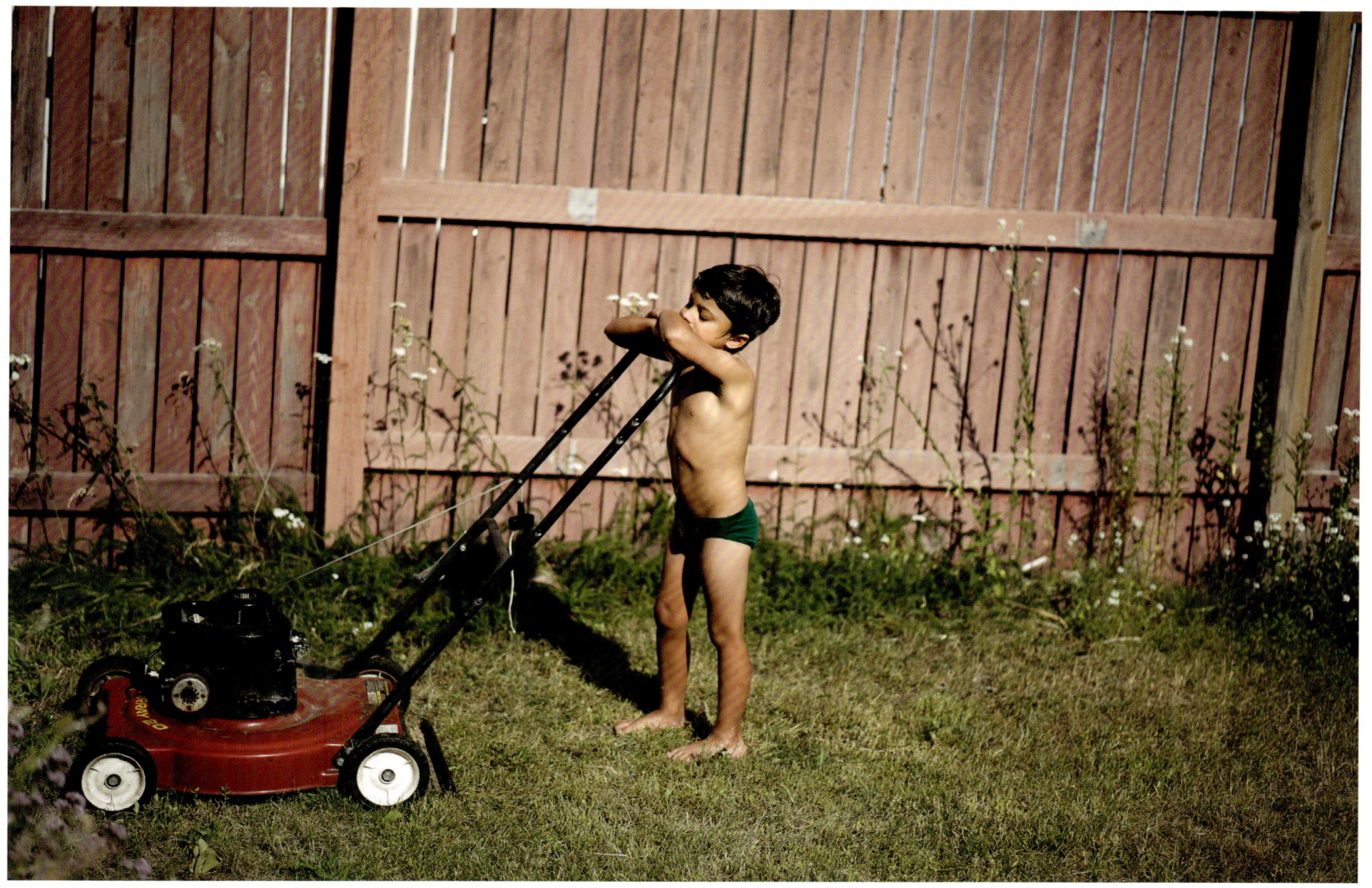

Spring flowers, blooming

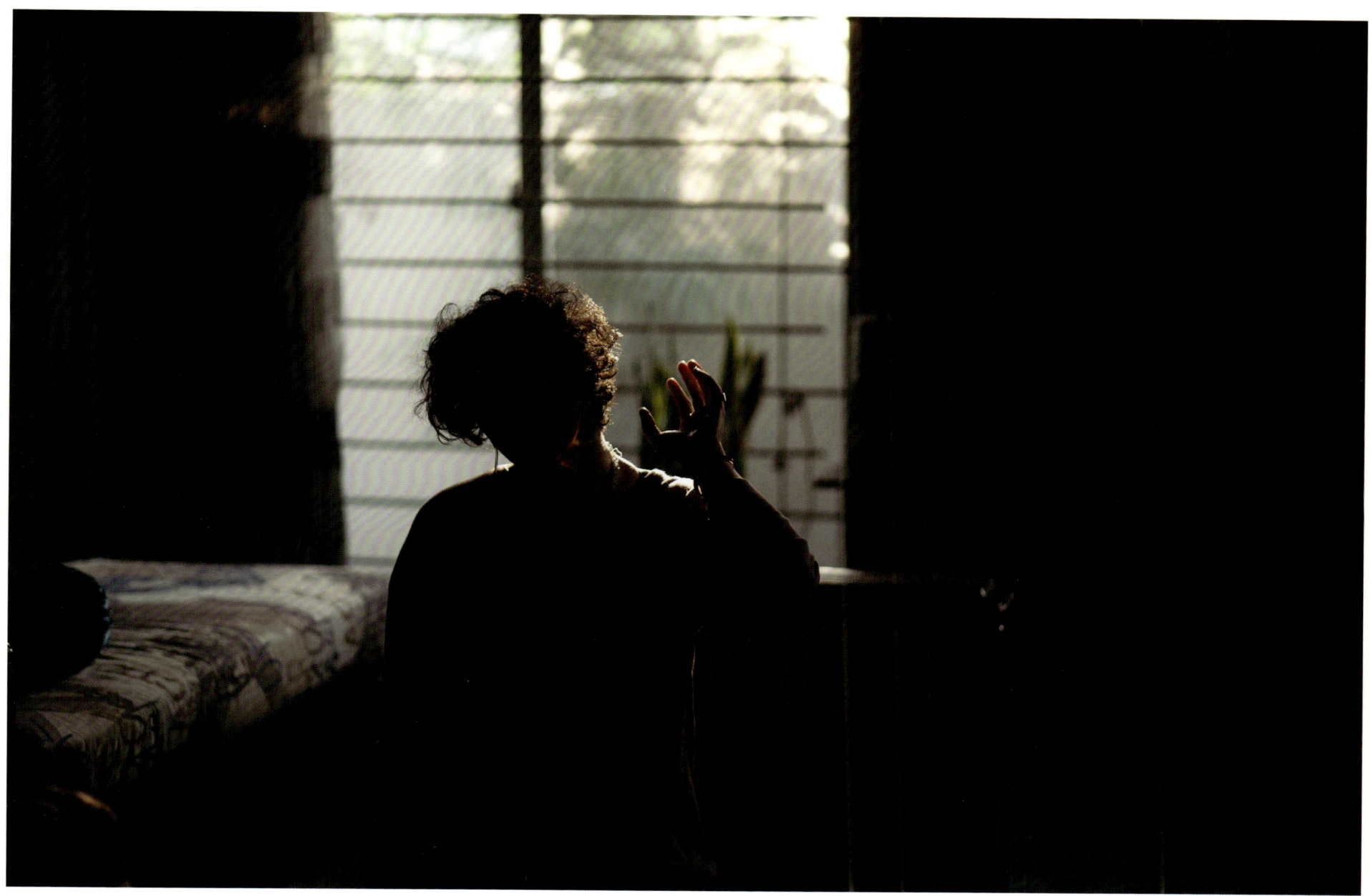

Home, away

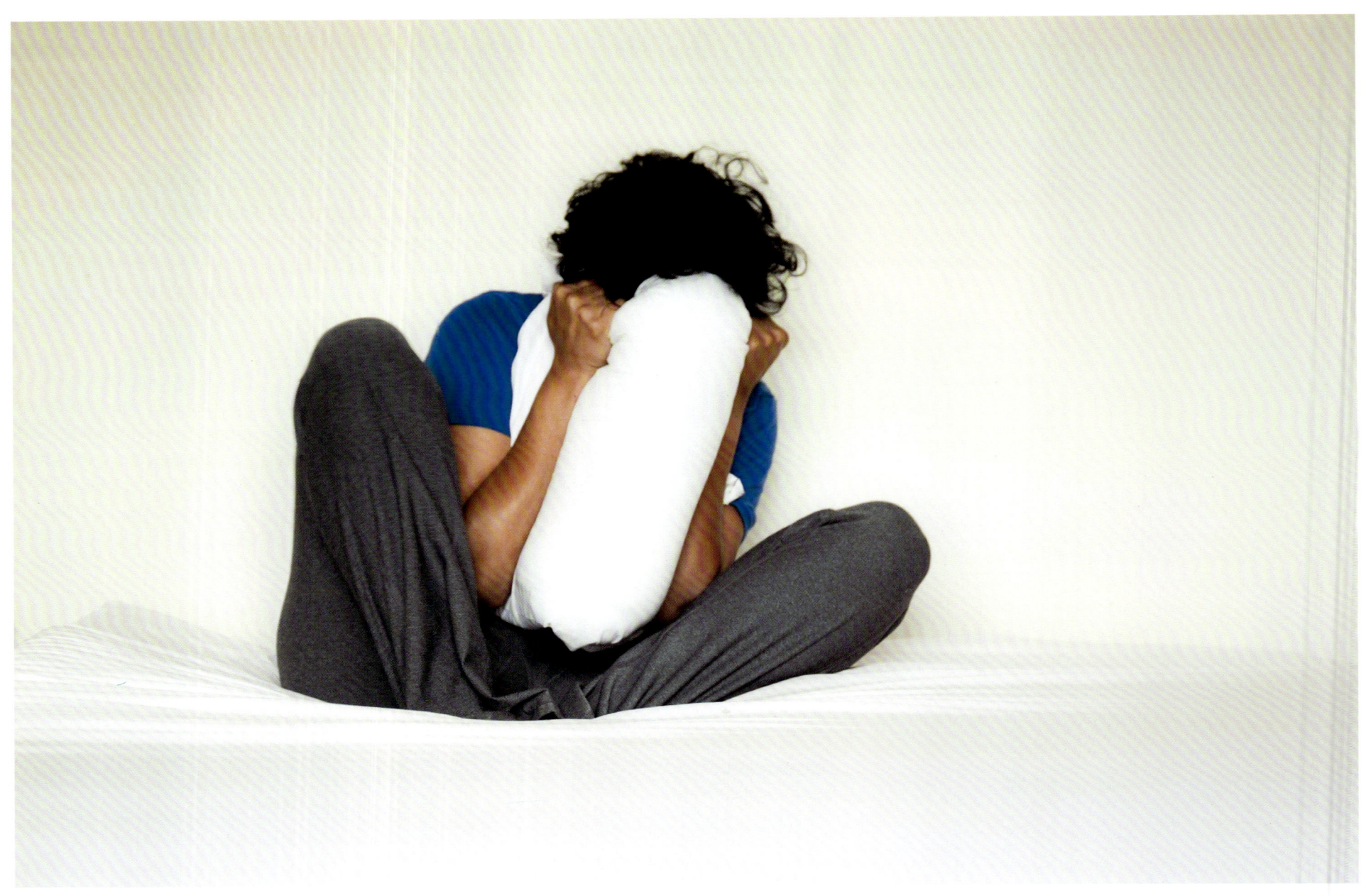

Where is that time?

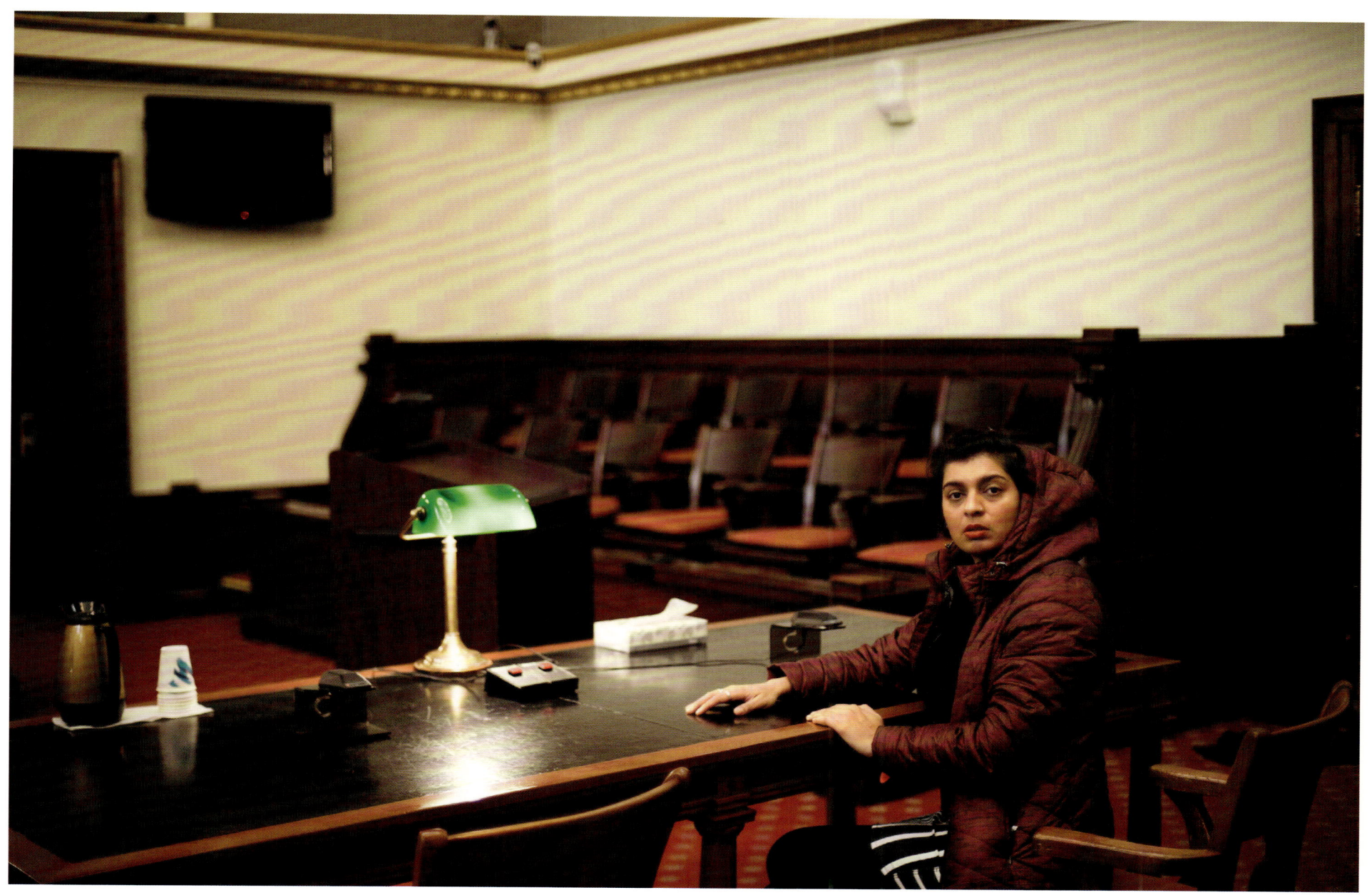

Why do they get to decide?

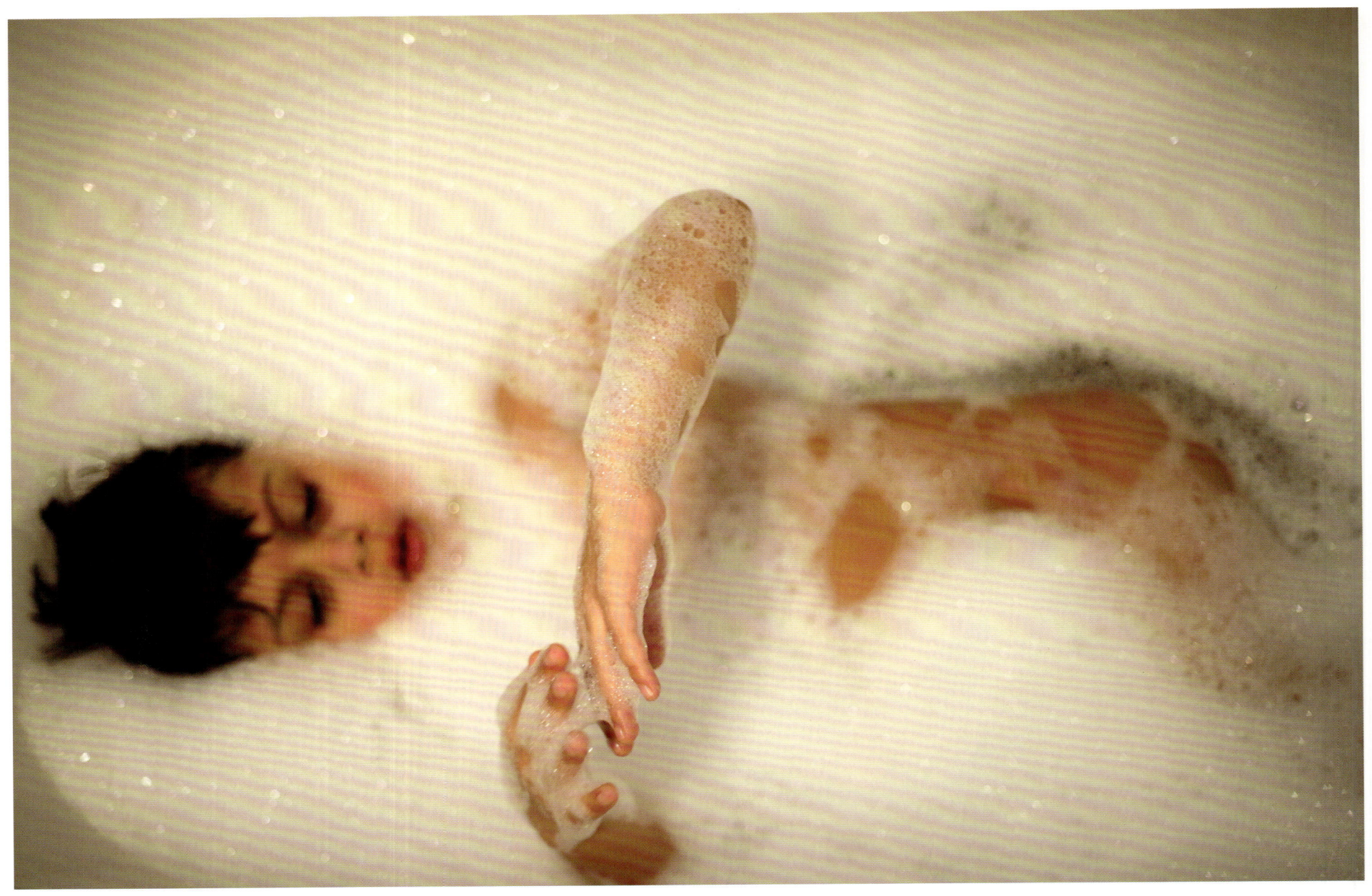

As I close my eyes

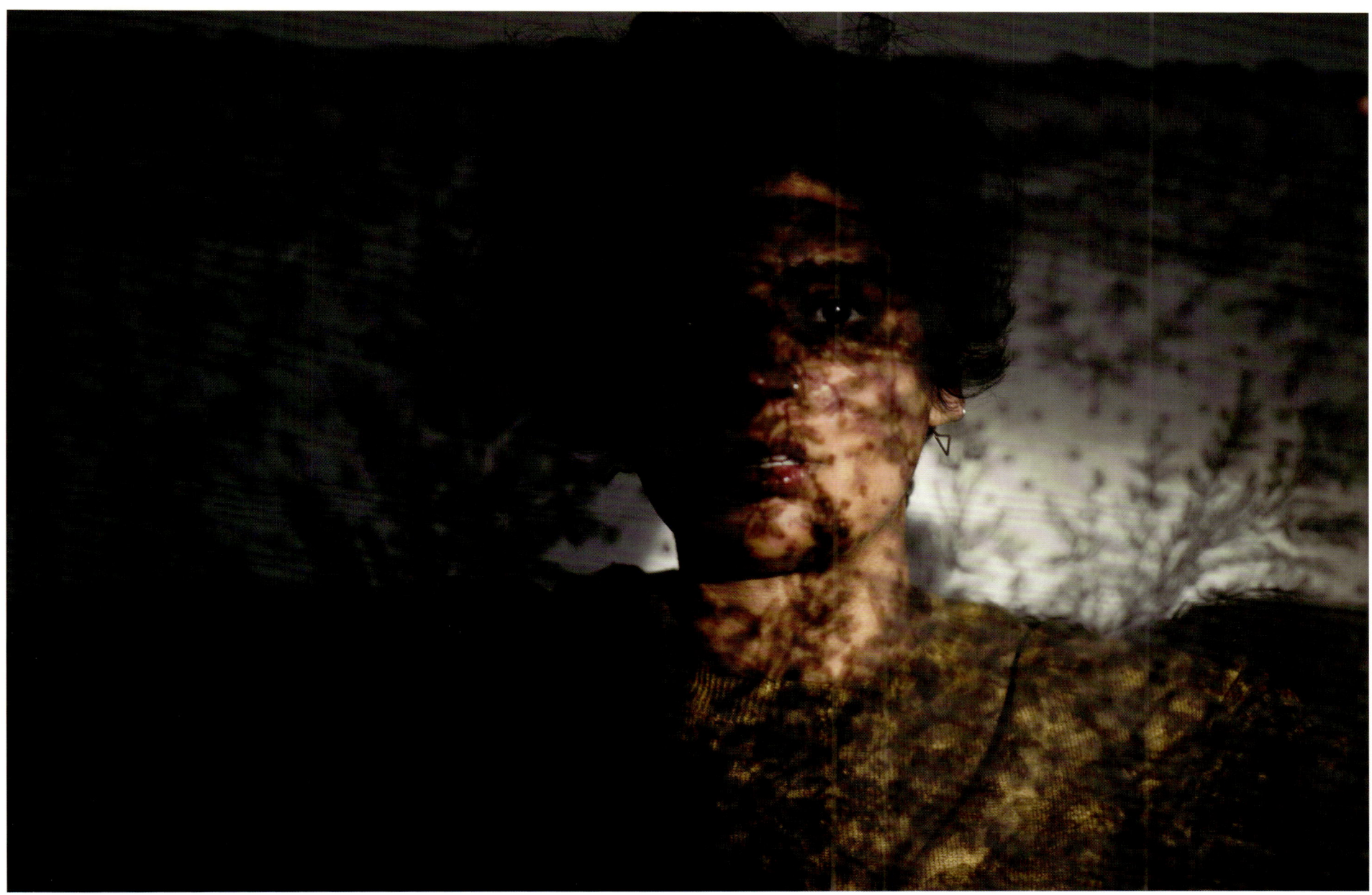

Becoming

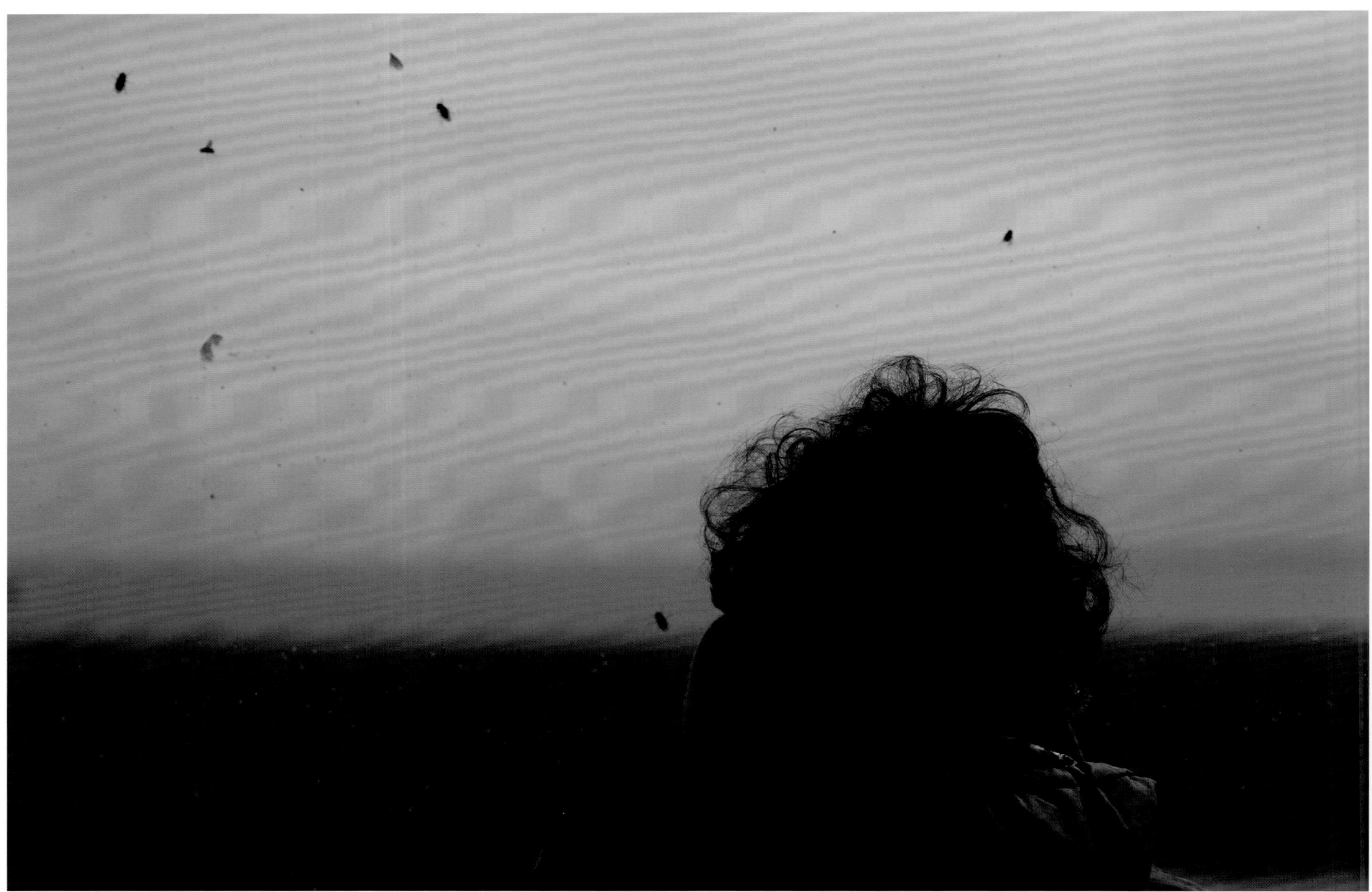

Without you

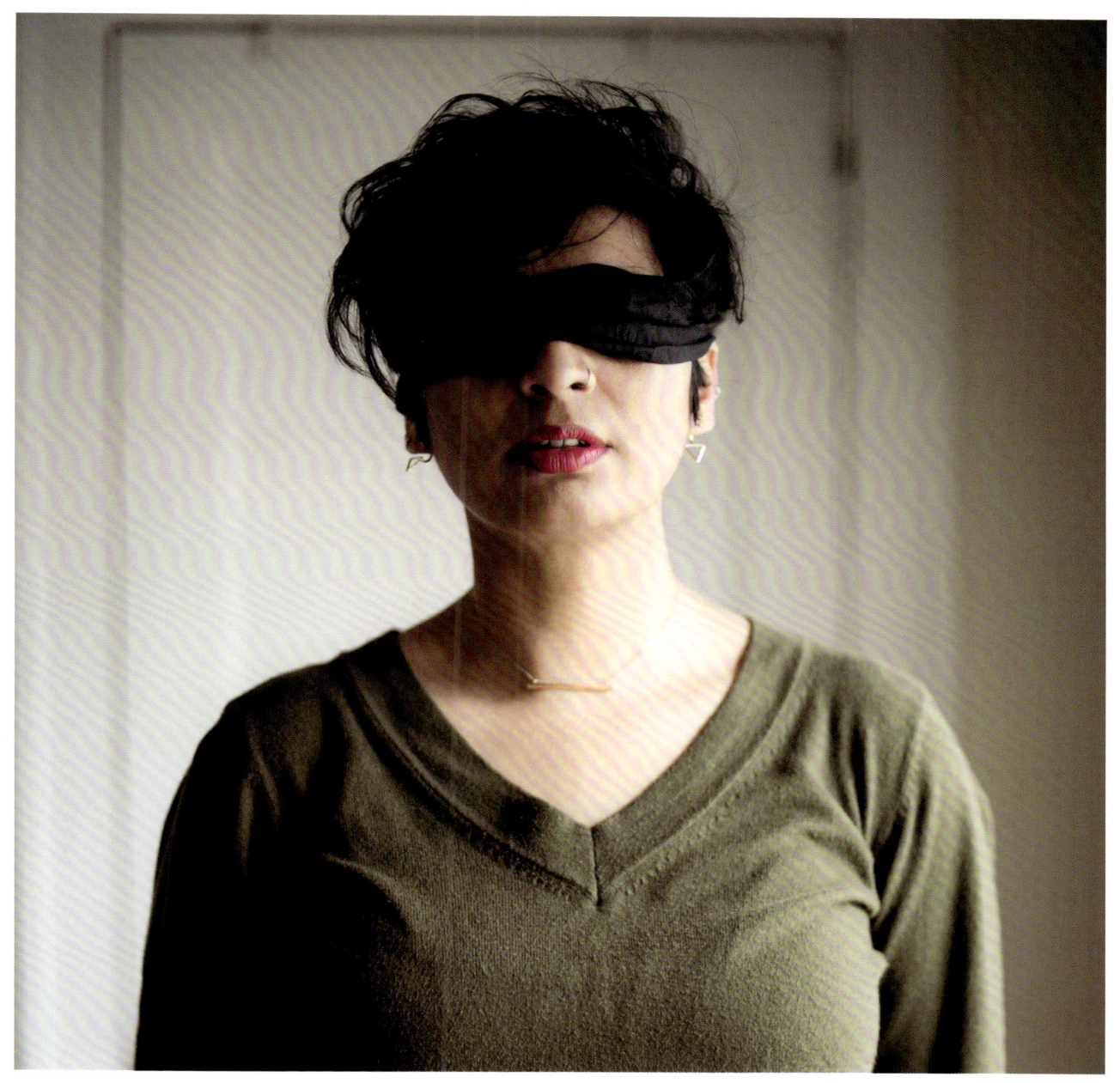

Blurring into oblivion

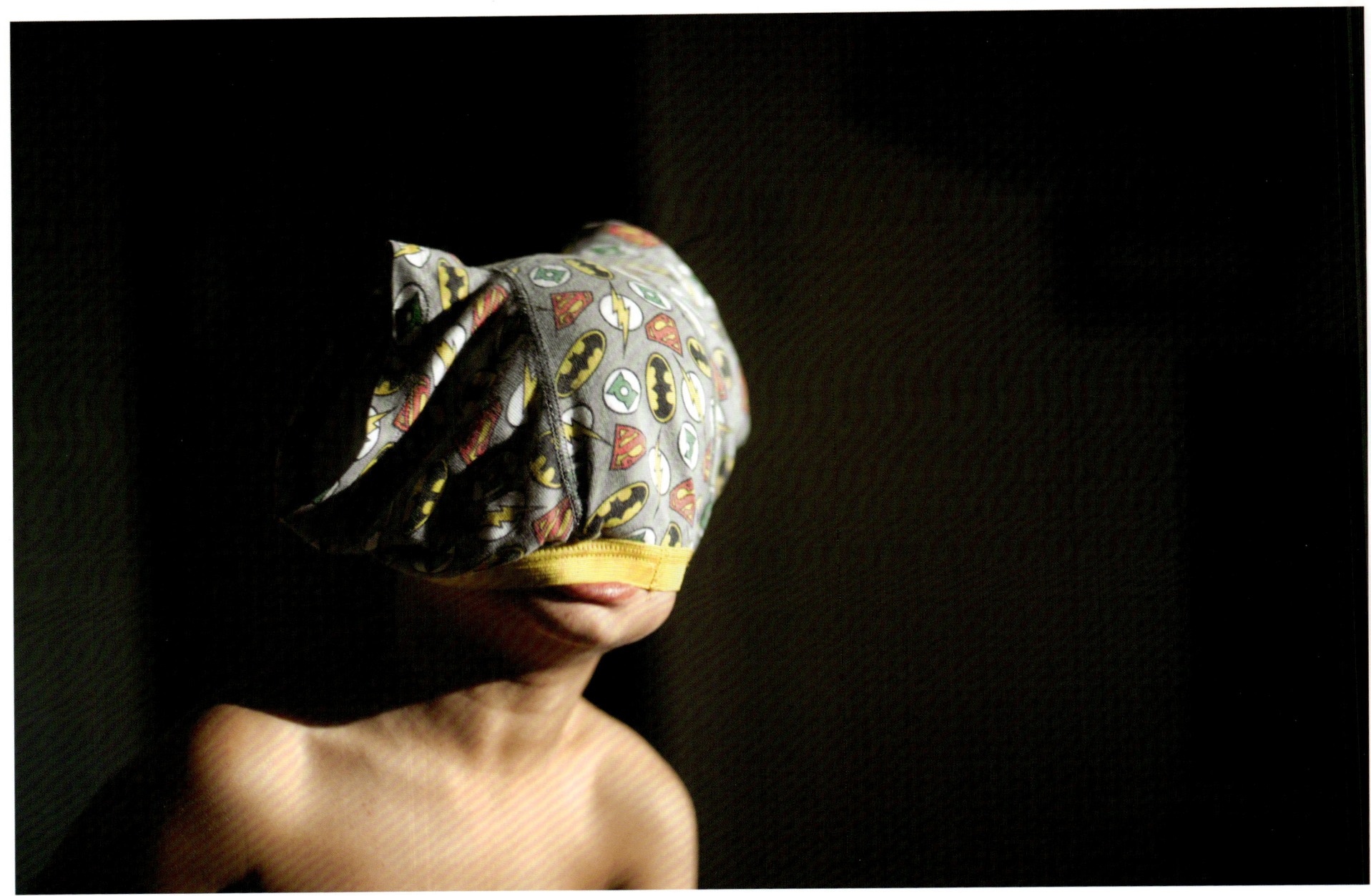

Light, falling

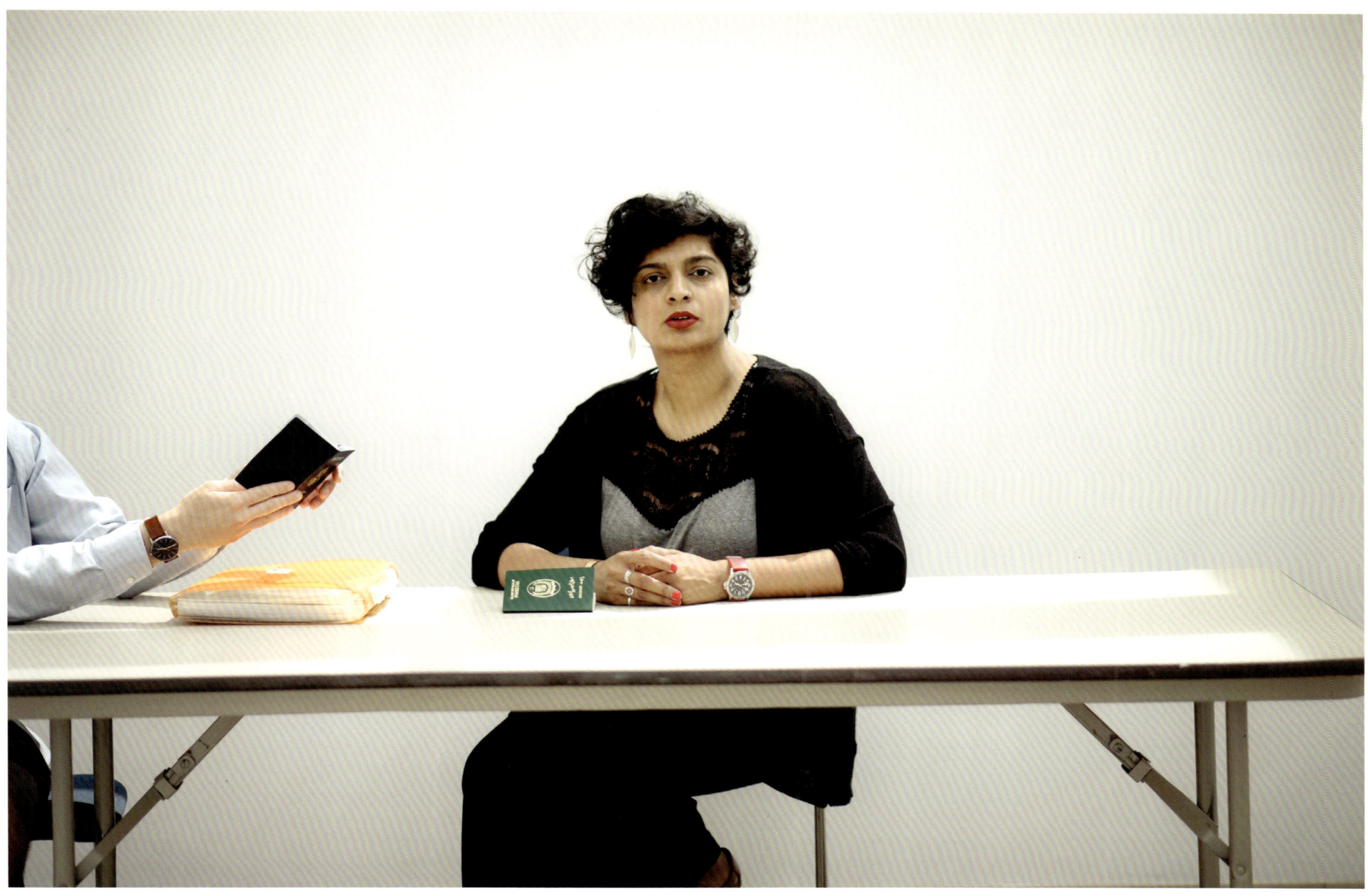

The sun will go down

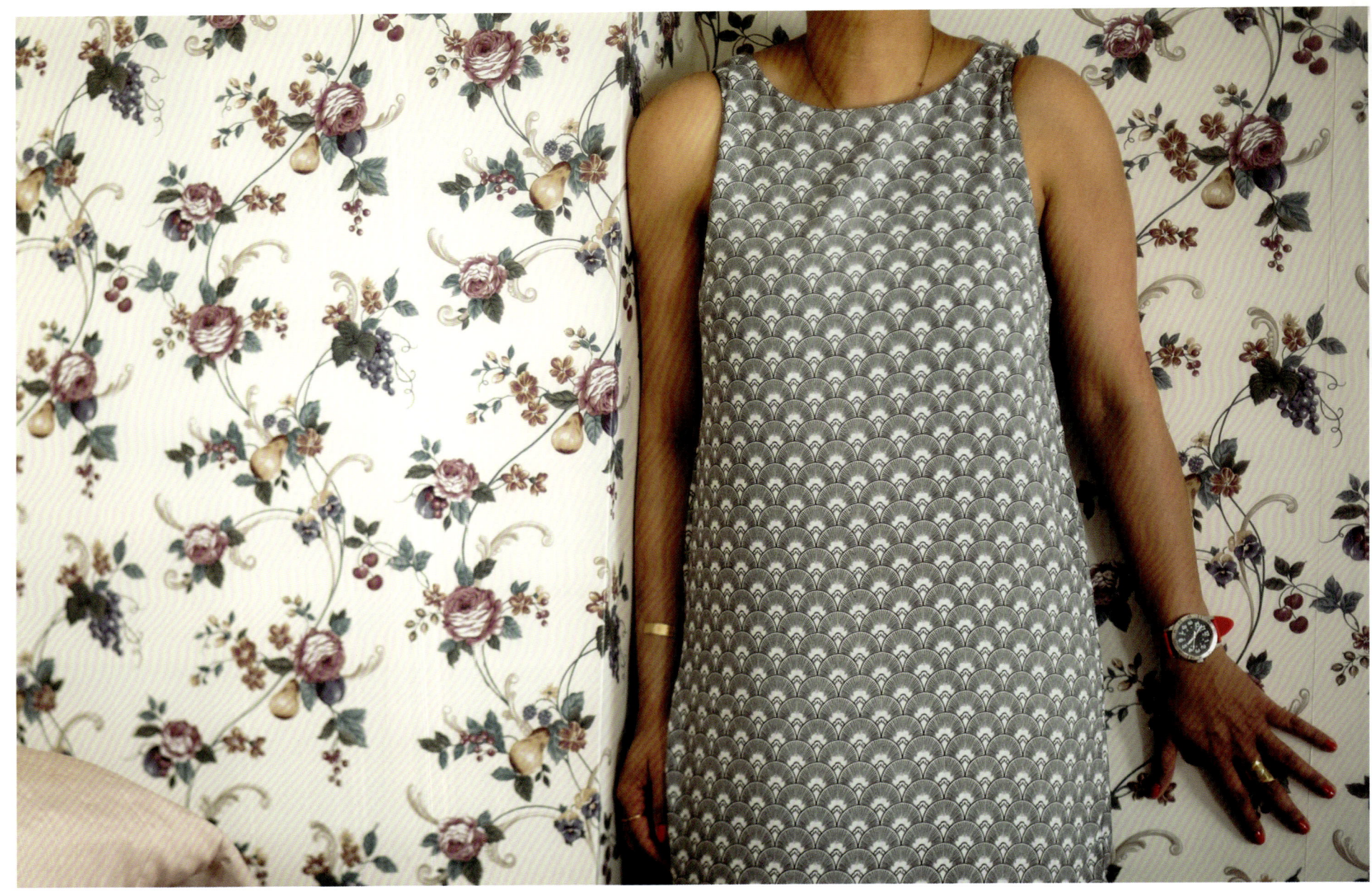

Unfamiliar, a hope

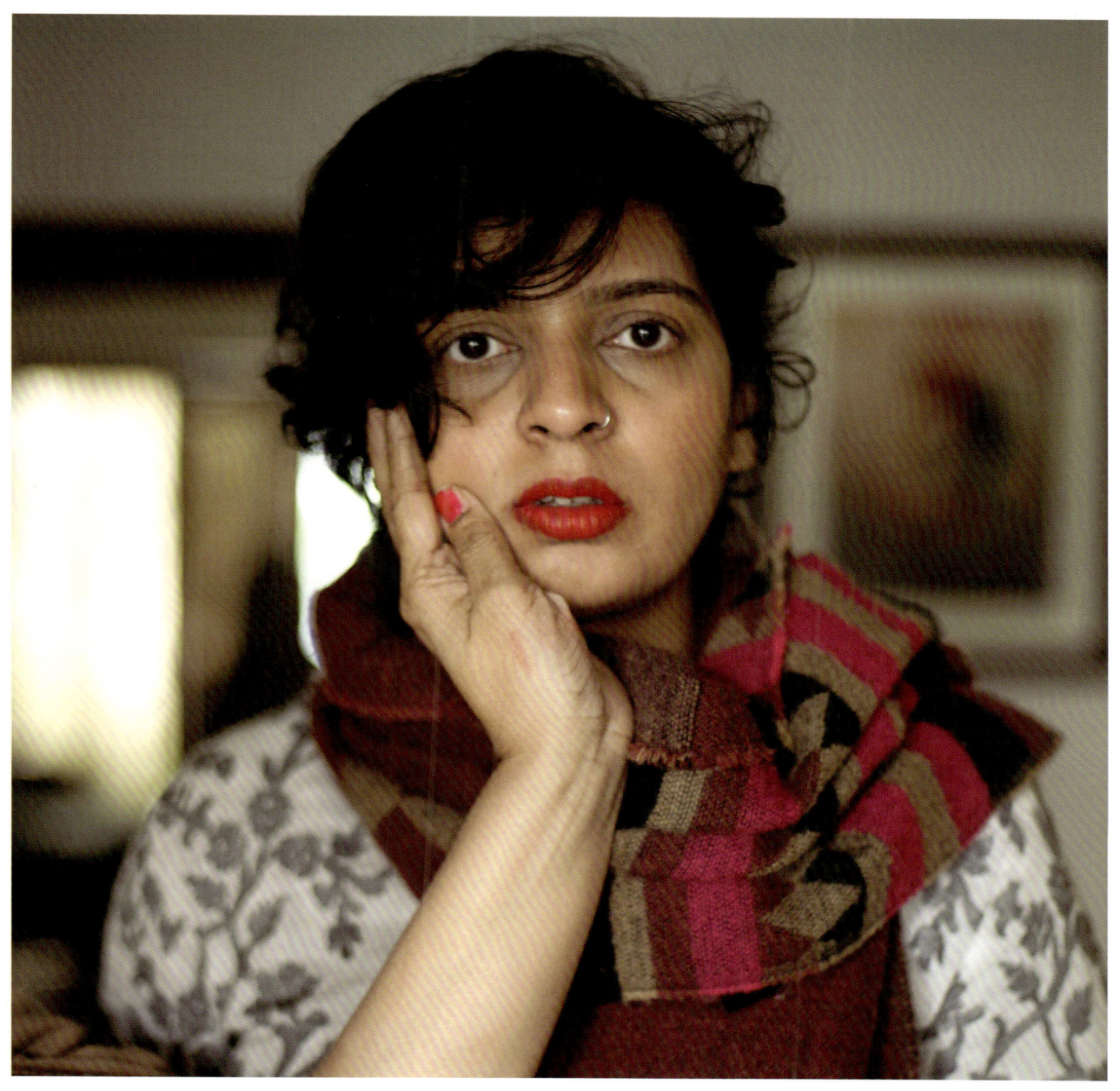

Breathing again

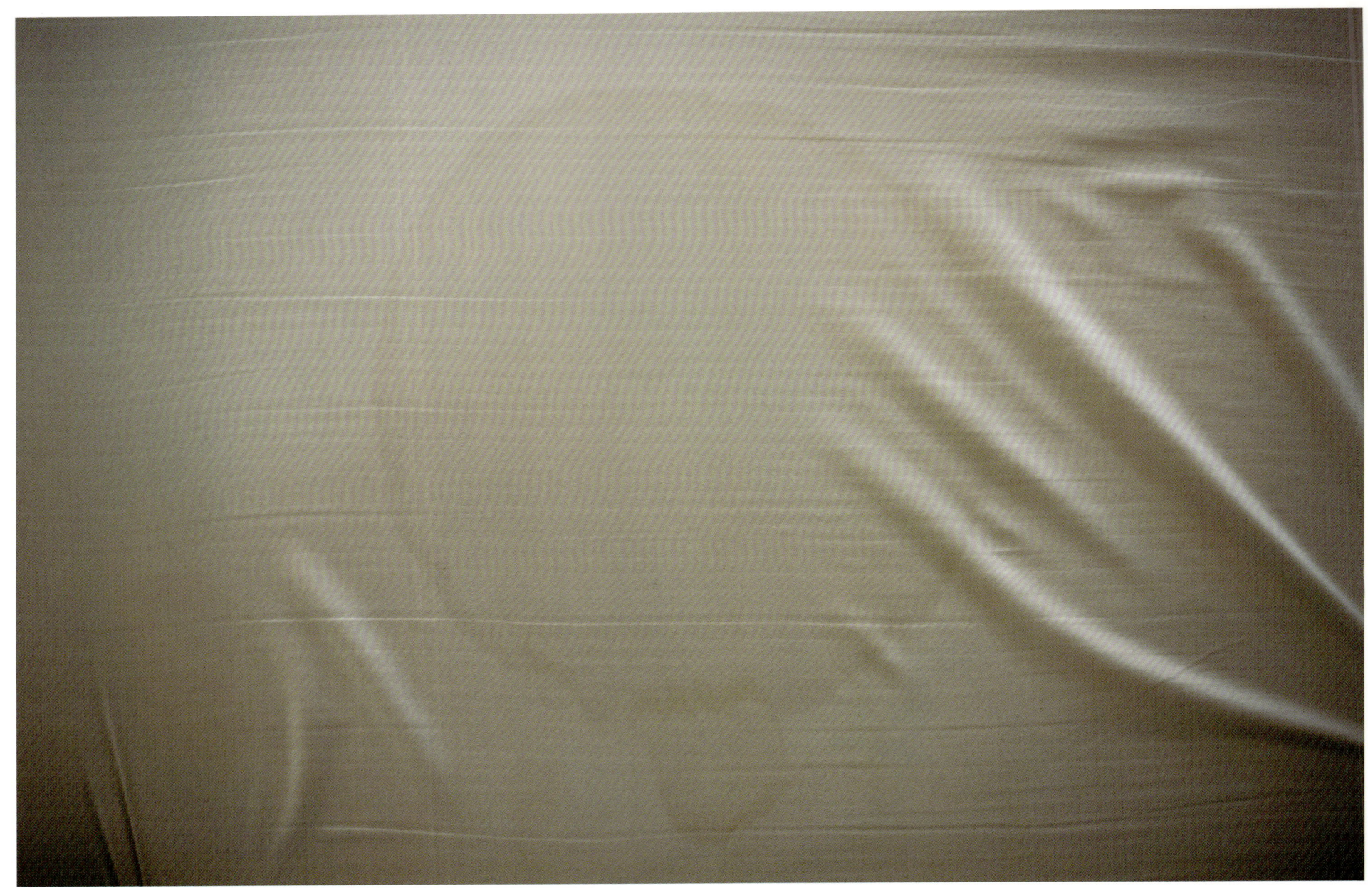

The morning routine

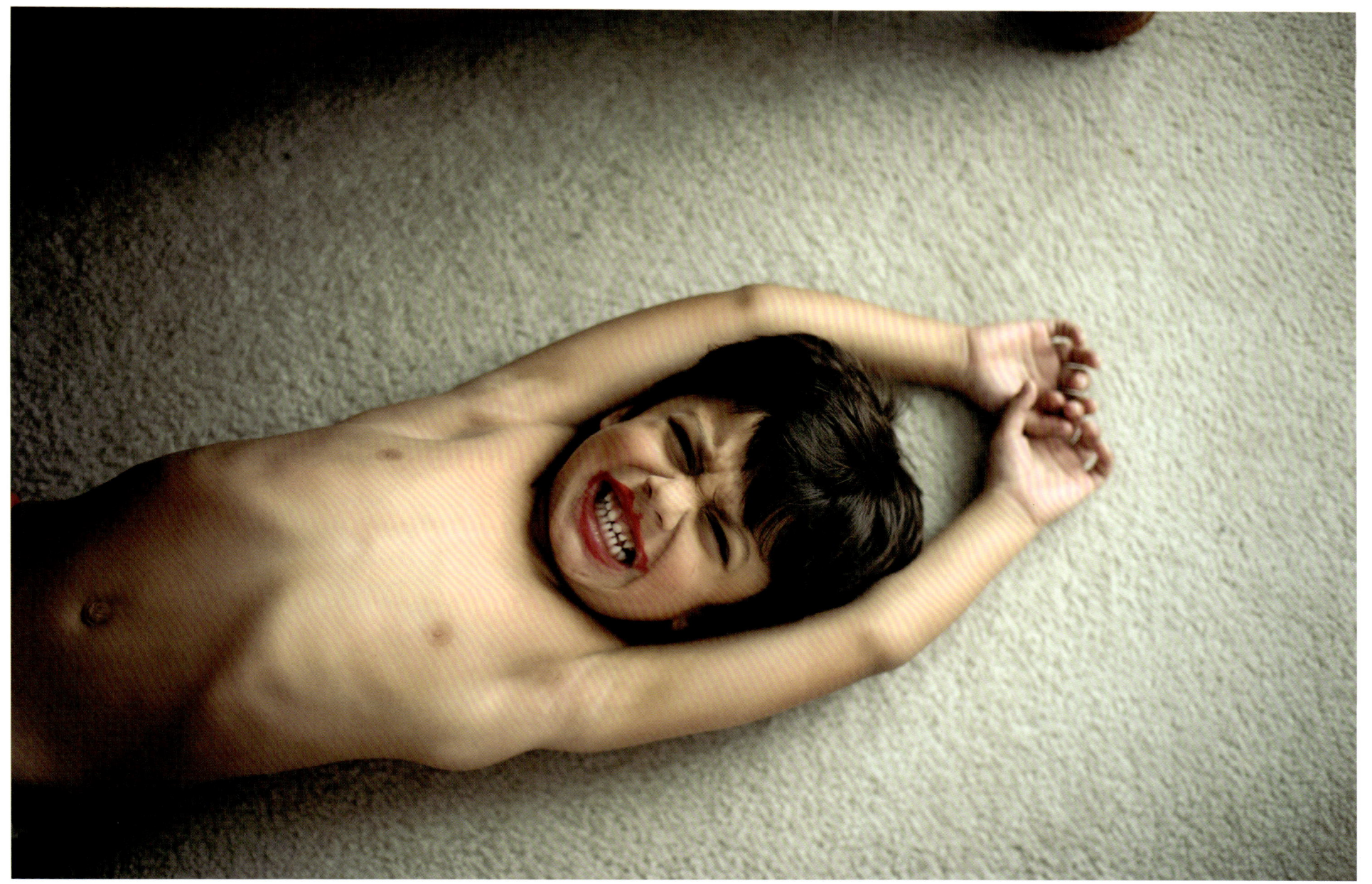

There is nothing to explain

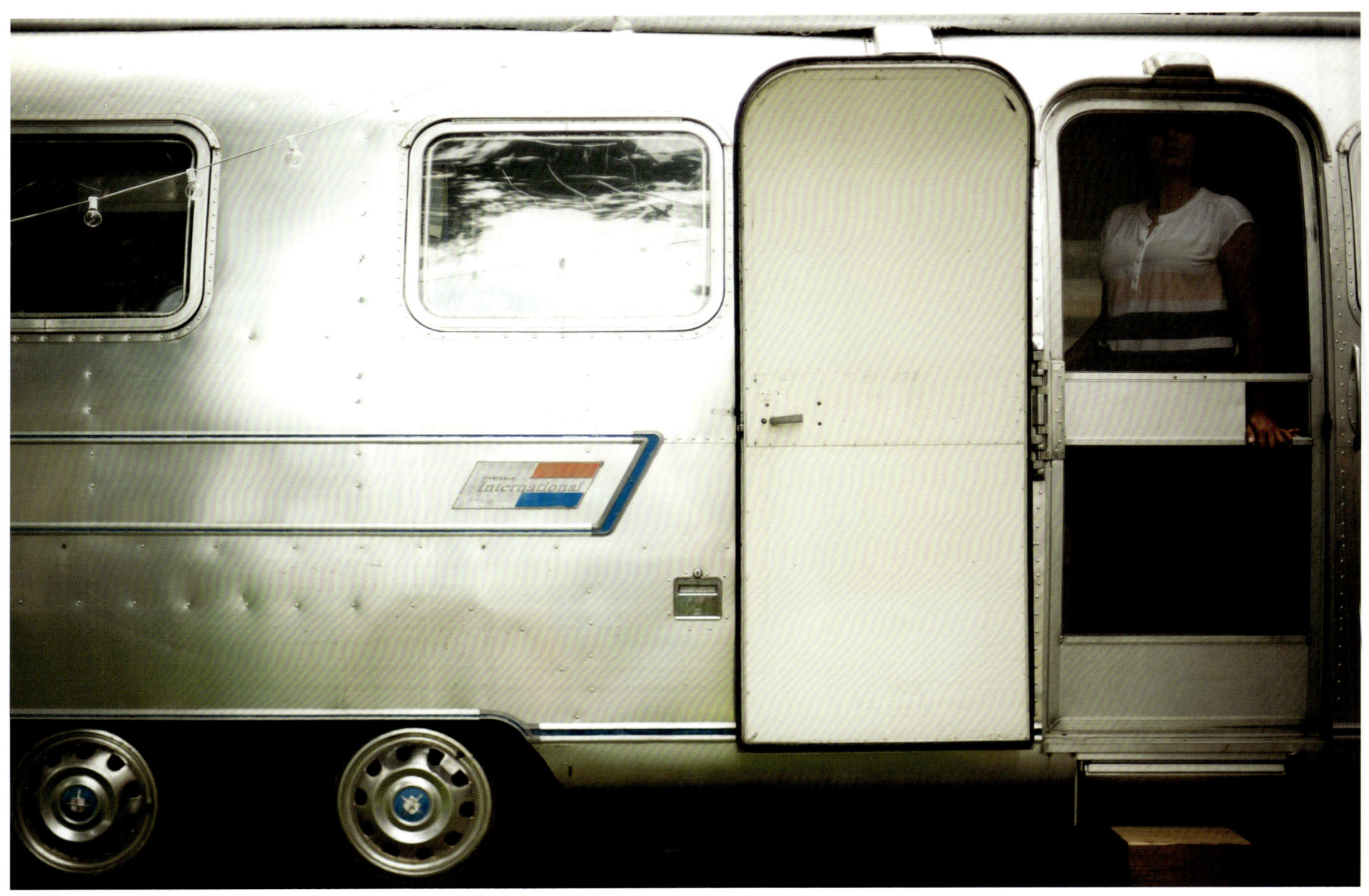

Surrounded by imitation

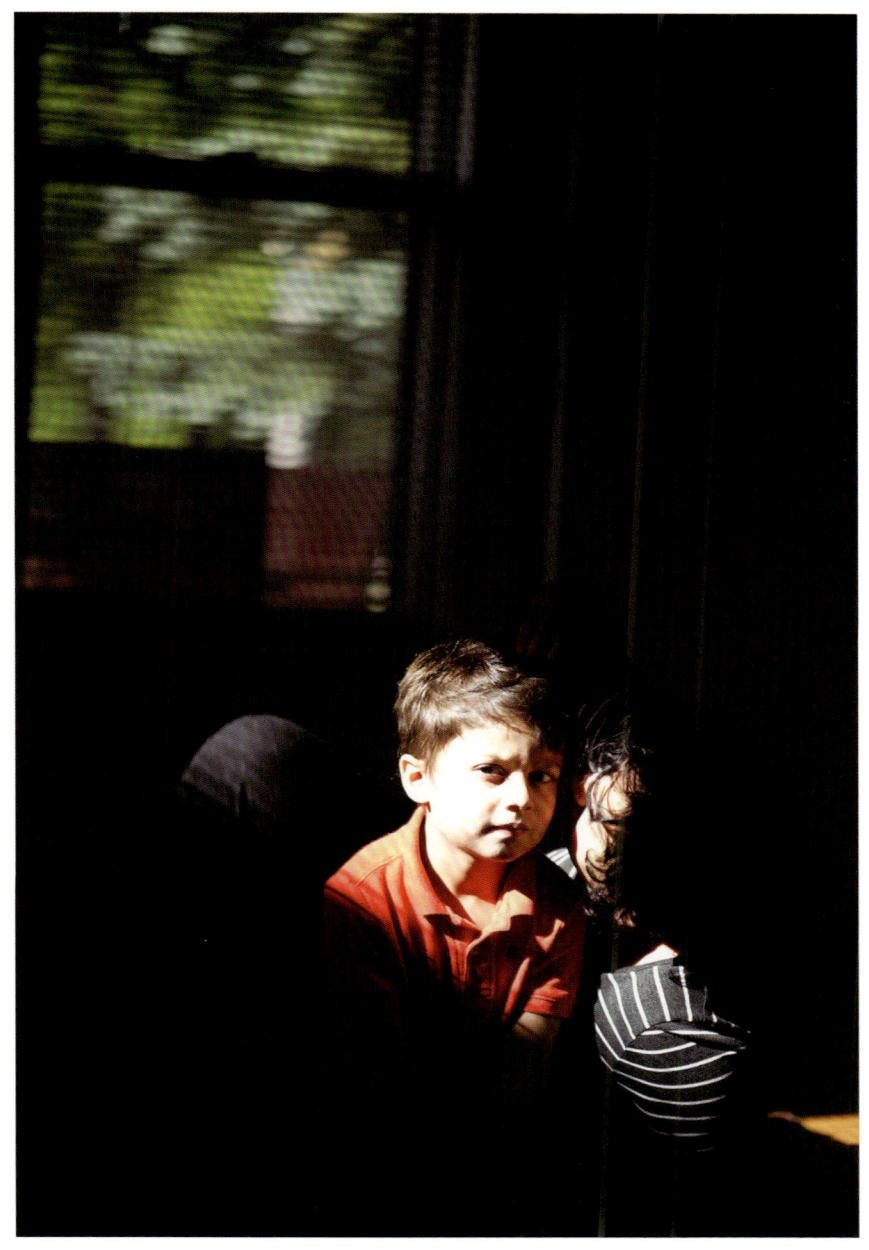

Whispering secrets

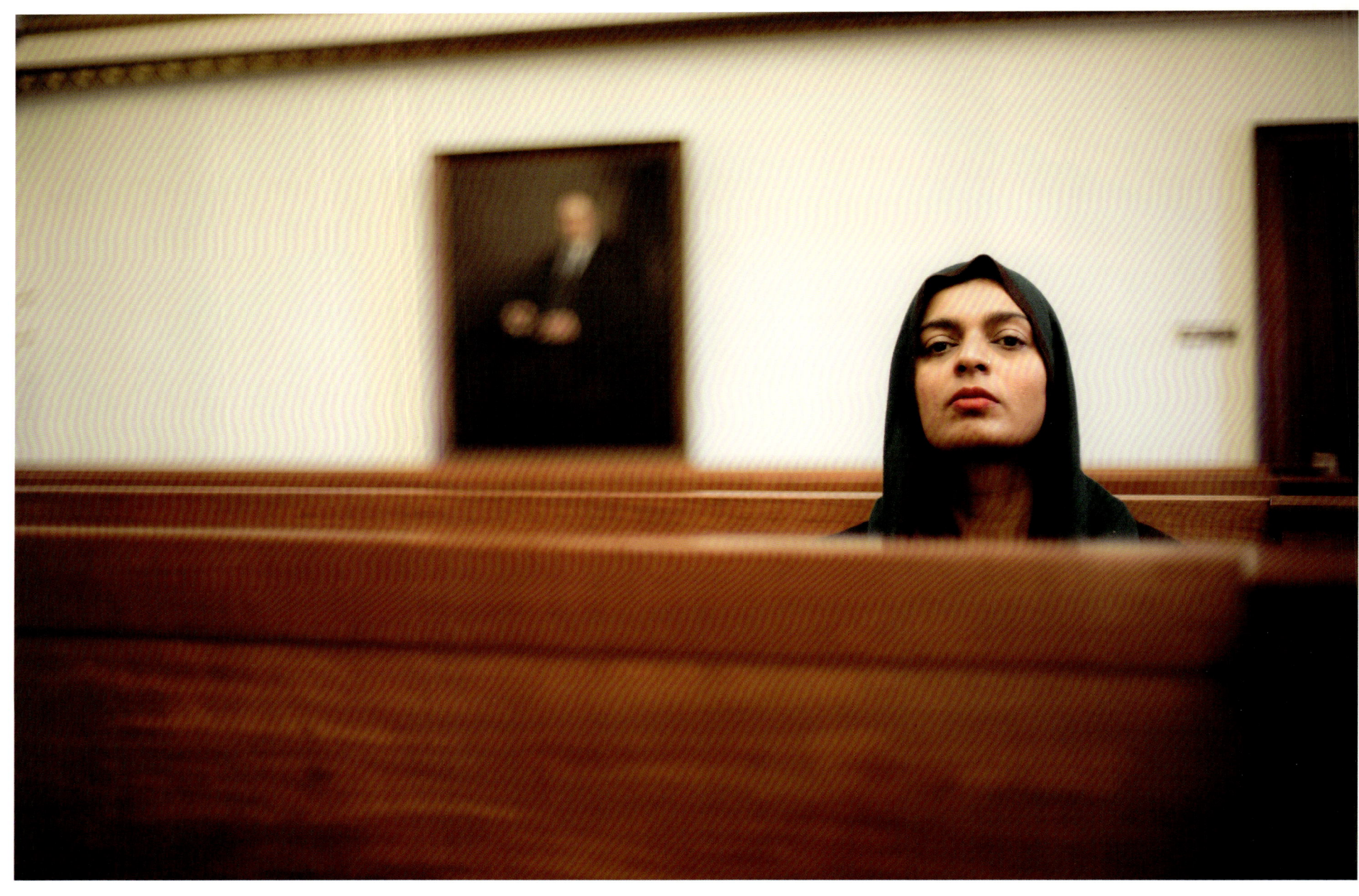

A number, not a name

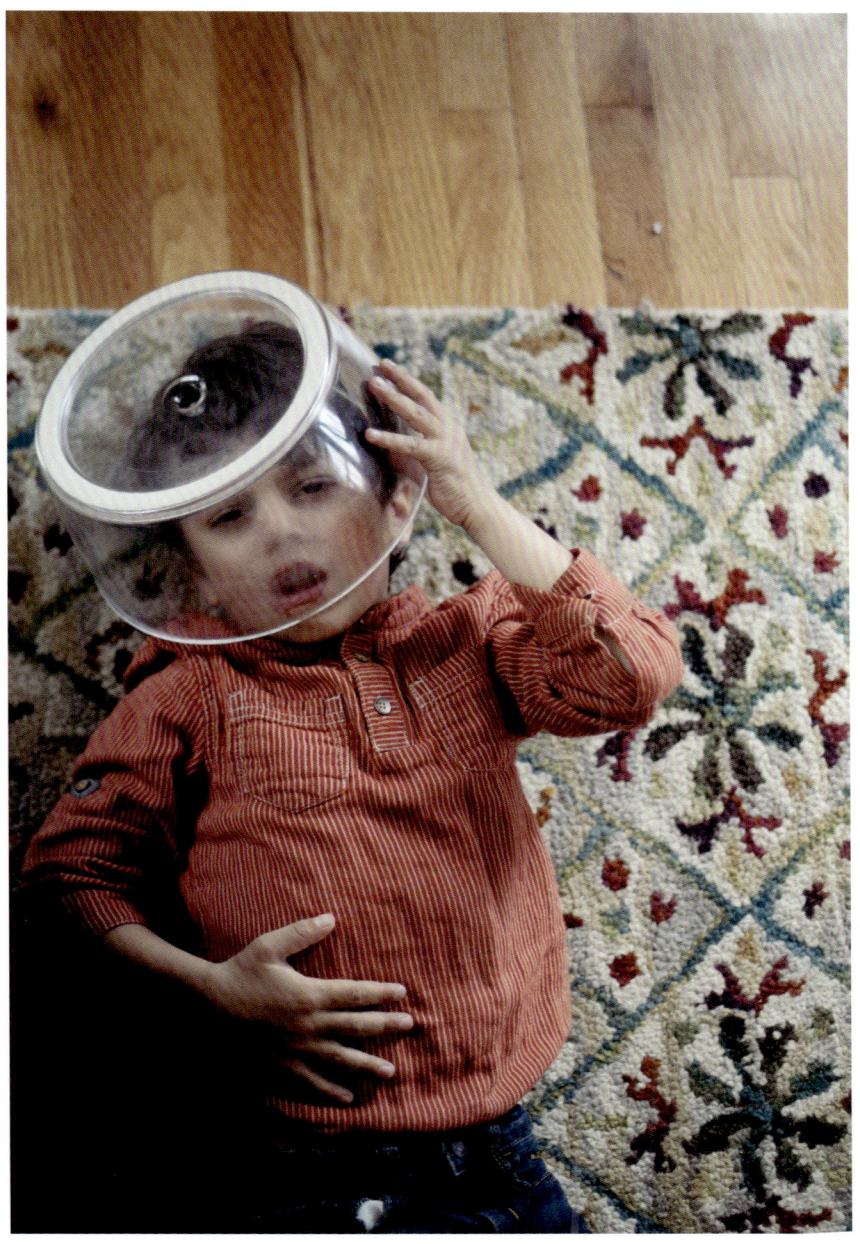

Seeing the breath

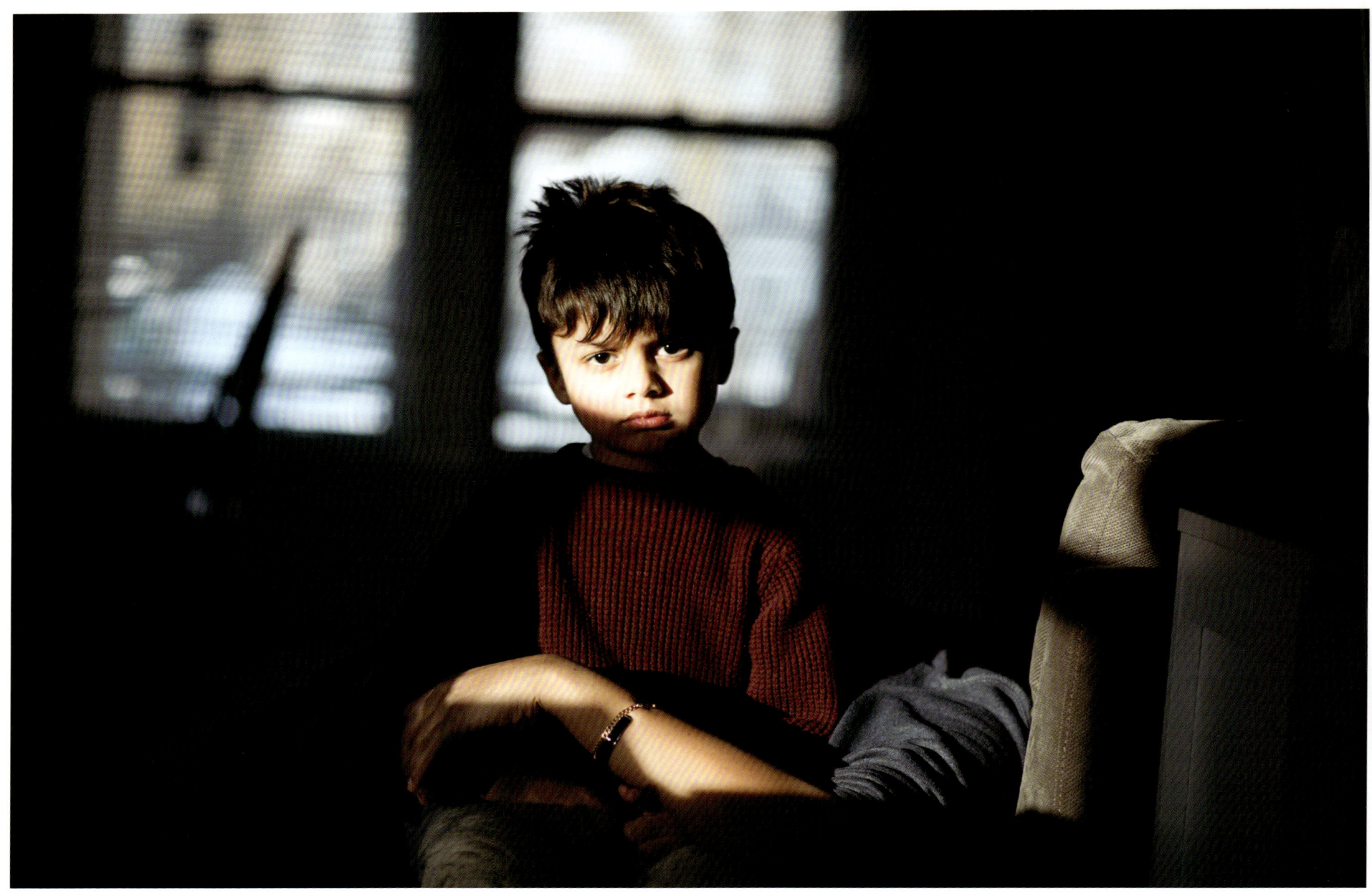

As the axis tilts

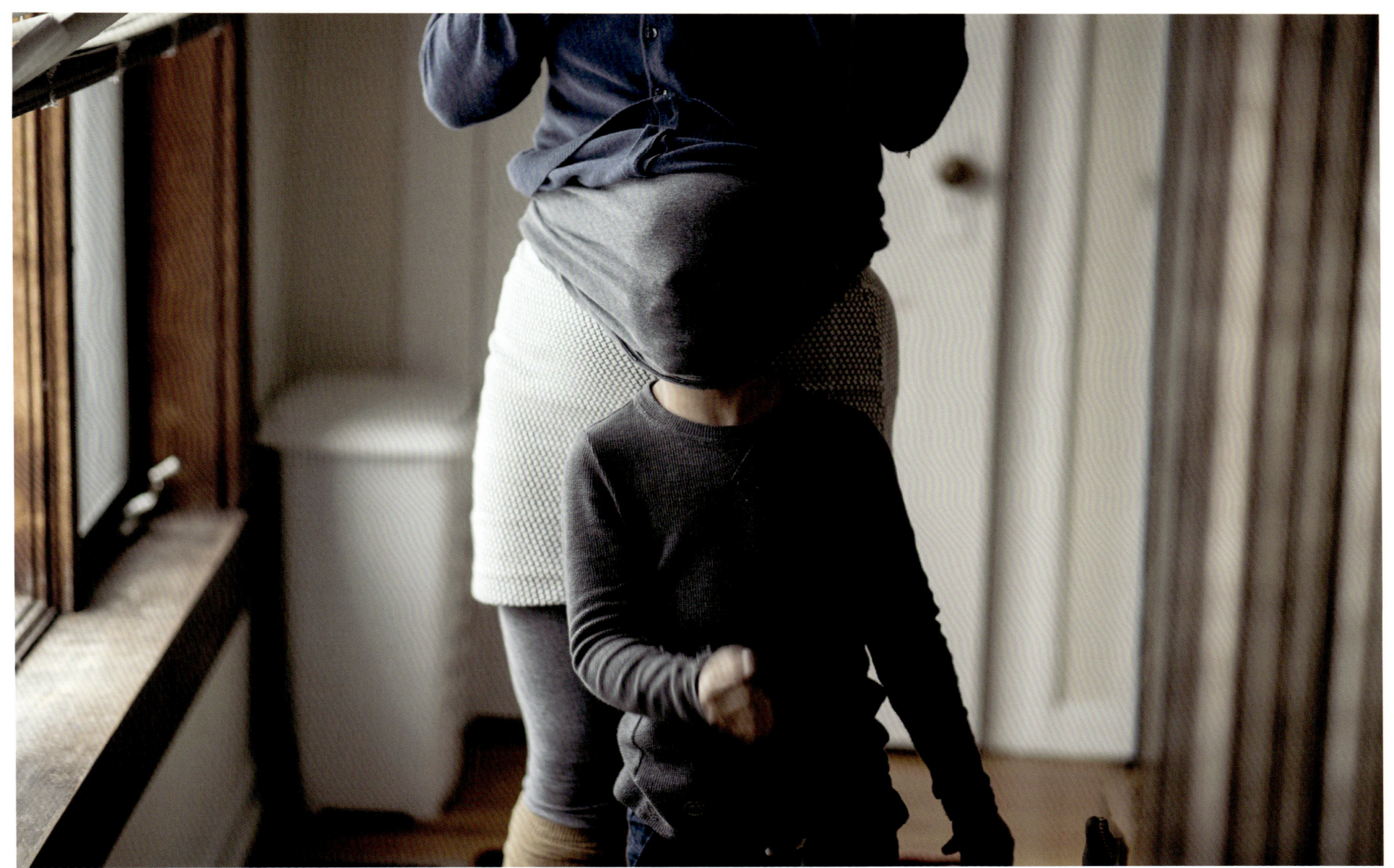

Of me, forever

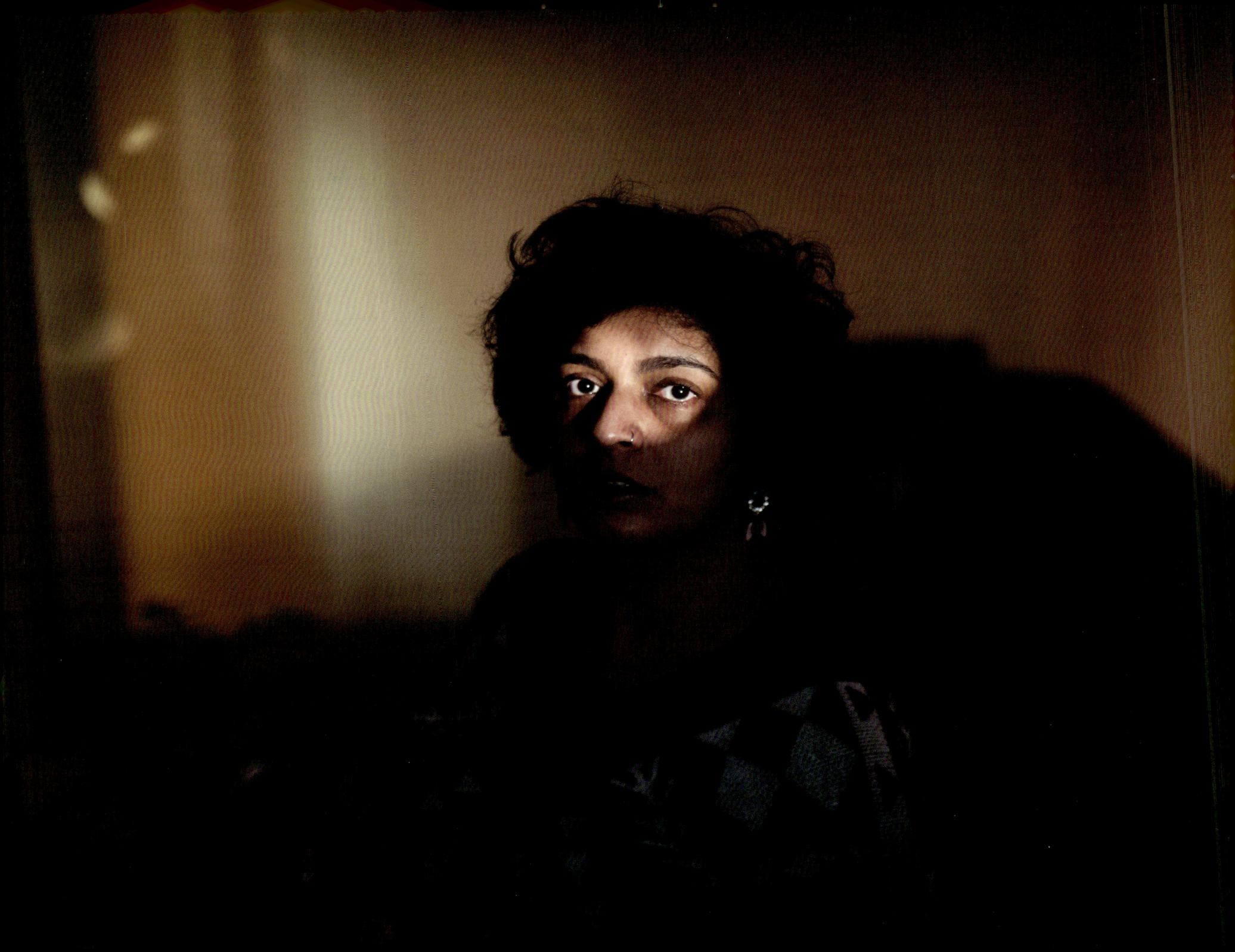

It is slipping from my fingers